STECK-VAUGHN

CRITICAL THINKING

Reading, Thinking, and Reasoning Skills

Teacher's Edition

Authors

Don Barnes
Professor of Education
Ball State University; Muncie, Indiana

Arlene Burgdorf
Former Resource Consultant
Hammond Indiana Public Schools

L. Stanley Wenck
Professor of Educational Psychology
Ball State University; Muncie, Indiana

Consultant

Gloria Sesso
Supervisor of Social Studies
Half Hollow Hills School District; Dix Hills, New York

LEVEL

A	B	C	D	**E**	F

STECK-VAUGHN
ELEMENTARY • SECONDARY • ADULT • LIBRARY
A Harcourt Company

www.steck-vaughn.com

TABLE OF CONTENTS

ISBN 0-8114-6610-8

12 13 795 09 08

Teach critical thinking skills in 5 simple steps!

Steck-Vaughn Critical Thinking

CRITICAL THINKING

Up-to-date, exciting, and effective

- **Each unit focuses on one stage of *Bloom's Taxonomy!*** Each book addresses knowing, understanding, applying, analyzing, synthesizing, and evaluating. (Levels 1 and 2 focus on only the first four stages.)
- **Inviting new unit openers!** Arouse curiosity and lead students into units with a good attitude for learning.
- **Lessons address one skill at a time!** Students master each skill before they move on to the next.
- **"Extending Your Skills" section at the end of each unit!** Brief, two-page reviews provide a convenient mastery check.
- **Six-book sequential program!** Students' critical thinking skills improve as their reading level increases.
- **At-home blackline master for each unit!** Involves parents in reinforcing new knowledge.
- **Exciting presentation!** Students are motivated by the variety of new and challenging activities and current, level-appropriate illustrations.

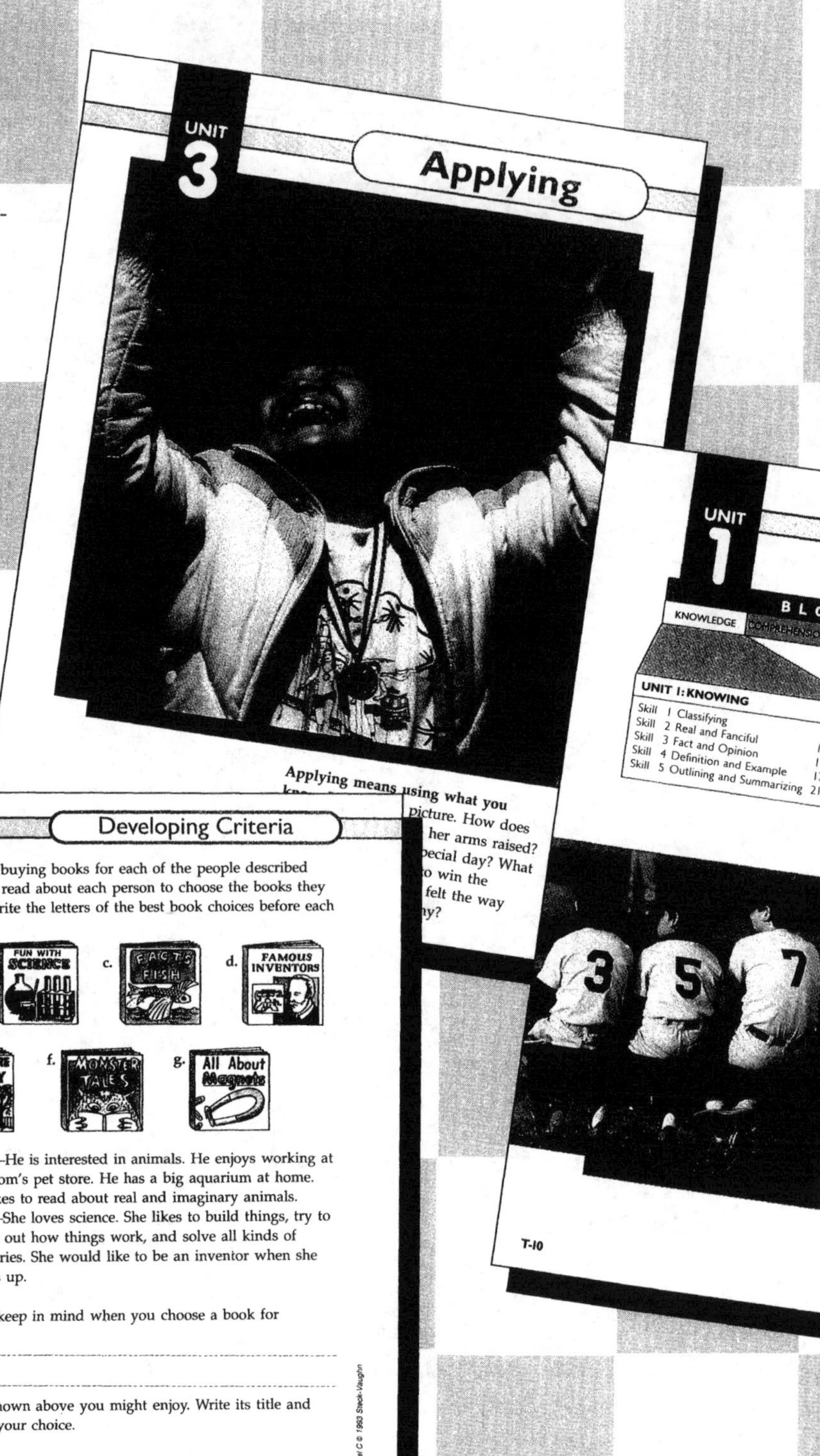

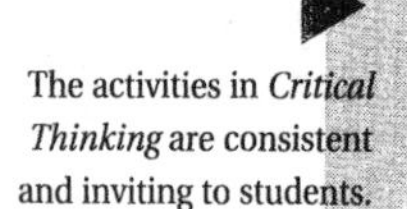

The activities in *Critical Thinking* are consistent and inviting to students.

SKILL 31 — Developing Criteria

A. Imagine that you are buying books for each of the people described below. Use what you read about each person to choose the books they would enjoy most. Write the letters of the best book choices before each name.

1. ________ Alex—He is interested in animals. He enjoys working at his mom's pet store. He has a big aquarium at home. He likes to read about real and imaginary animals.
2. ________ Sara—She loves science. She likes to build things, try to figure out how things work, and solve all kinds of mysteries. She would like to be an inventor when she grows up.

B. What things do you keep in mind when you choose a book for yourself? ____________________

____

Decide which book shown above you might enjoy. Write its title and give two reasons for your choice.

____

____

Name ____________________

114

Classifying

SKILL 1 PAGES 6-10

STEP ONE Define the Skill
Discuss with your pupils the meaning of *classifying*: **grouping things, people, or ideas because they are alike in some way.**

STEP TWO Identify the Steps
Explain to your students the steps they need to follow to classify any group of items, large or small:
1. Look at the items and decide which are alike in some way.
2. Place the like things together in one group.
3. Give a name to each group.
4. See if you can classify the items in one group into smaller groups.

STEP THREE Demonstrate the Skill
Ask pupils to watch and listen as you classify a group of items, following Step Two. **SUGGESTION:** On the board, write the names of different animals in random order. Then write three numbered categories—*pets, farm animals, wild animals*. Number animals by category, explaining why you are grouping them this way. Show pupils that one category may also be divided into smaller categories or be part of larger categories—for example, poodles and beagles are kinds of pet dogs; pet dogs, along with some pets, farm animals, and wild animals are furry animals.

STEP FOUR Practice the Skill
Use pages 6–10. See *Teacher Note* on each page.

STEP FIVE Provide Feedback
Discuss pupils' answers. **METACOGNITION:** Ask pupils to describe what they did. You may need to ask: **How did you decide whether certain things were alike? What did you look at or think about? How did you decide what name to give each group?**

ENRICHMENT ACTIVITIES

Present several categories, such as things that have wheels and things that grow. Challenge groups of pupils to list as many things for each category as they can in a certain amount of time.

Have pupils build a word web indicating how an item such as scissors may be used. Angled out from the word *scissors* might be *haircut, surgery, sewing, and cut paper.*

Classify animals according to where they might live. Help pupils conclude that some animals may live in several different areas. A horse might be at a circus, on a farm, or in the wild; a snake might be on a farm and in a jungle.

Real and Fanciful

SKILL 2 PAGES 11-12

STEP ONE Define the Skill
Discuss with your pupils the meaning of knowing the difference between *real and fanciful:* **knowing the difference between things that are real and things that are only imagined.**

STEP TWO Identify the Steps
Explain to your pupils the steps they need to follow to tell the difference between real and fanciful:
1. Look at a picture carefully or read the words carefully.
2. Decide whether the picture or the words tell about something that can really happen or something that can only be imagined.

STEP THREE Demonstrate the Skill
Ask pupils to watch and listen as you show the difference between real and fanciful, following Step Two. **SUGGESTION:** Write two sample sentences on the board—*My family lives in a brown brick house* and *My family lives in a magician's mirror*. Point out that the sentences are the same except for the final phrases. The last phrase in the first sentence describes a place where a family really could live; the last phrase in the second sentence does not. Therefore, the first statement could be real; the second is imaginary, or fanciful.

STEP FOUR Practice the Skill
Use pages 11–12. See *Teacher Note* on each page.

STEP FIVE Provide Feedback
Discuss pupils' answers. **METACOGNITION:** Ask pupils to describe what they did. You may need to ask: **How did you decide which things were real and which were fanciful? How did you decide which statements were real and which were fanciful?**

Unit I **T-11**

Teach critical thinking skills in 5 simple steps

This is an all-new edition of *Steck-Vaughn Critical Thinking,* but one thing hasn't changed: the acclaimed 5-step lesson plan. This thorough, predictable instructional approach has helped thousands of students develop reading and reasoning skills that will serve them for a lifetime.

1 Define the Skill
Discuss the meaning of classifying with your pupils: grouping ideas, objects, or people according to things they have in common.

2 Identify the Steps
Explain to your pupils the steps they need to follow to classify any group of items, large or small.

3 Demonstrate the Skill
Ask pupils to watch and listen as you classify a group of items, following the four steps.

4 Practice the Skill
Use pages 6-10 to give pupils an opportunity to practice classifying

5 Provide Feedback
Have pupils correct and discuss their answers.

The 5-step lesson plan is back!

Knowing

AXONOMY

ANALYSIS | SYNTHESIS | EVALUATION

VLEDGE is the term used in Bloom's
my for the first stage in cognitive
ment. This starting point includes both
isition of information and the ability
the information when needed.

rs of this program have identified the
skills as being particularly helpful in
g Bloom's first stage:

fying
ninating Between Real and Fanciful
ninating Between Fact and Opinion
inating Between Definition and
e
g and Summarizing

procedures for teaching each of these
These lesson plans will help you use
vith ease as you incorporate *thinking*
r teaching day. Enrichment activities
y each lesson will help your students
ly acquired thinking skills to a
ions.

as been completed, copy and
hool-Home Newsletter on

New and expanded teacher editions include a comprehensive introduction to each unit. Lesson pages are level appropriate and include stimulating enrichment activities to challenge students in different ways.

Bigger, better Teacher's Editions

- **At-home; enrichment activities!** Sixteen new pages per book include parent-involvement activities and three types of all-new enrichment activities.
- **Level-appropriate Teacher's Edition introductions!** Teachers can model lessons on an appropriate example at each level.
- **Comprehensive lesson plans!** Clarify instructional theories, goals, and mechanics.
- **Lessons written in conversational tone include examples which demonstrate each skill!** Teachers can present lessons right out of the book with minimal preparation.
- **Scope and Sequence charts!** Correlate skills to appropriate page numbers in each book.
- **Progress chart blackline master!** Allows teachers to record and monitor each pupil's achievements.

Thinker's Corner

SCHOOL—HOME NEWSLETTER

UNIT 4
ANALYZING

In the fourth unit of *Critical Thinking: Reading, Thinking, and Reasoning Skills,* your child has been studying the following skills:

- judging completeness
- relevance of information
- abstract or concrete
- logic of actions
- elements of a selection
- story logic
- recognizing fallacies

This newsletter is designed to provide an important link between home and school. You can support your child's learning habits by asking what he or she has learned in school and by discussing papers brought home. You may also wish to do some of the activities suggested in this newsletter.

What's Missing?
Have your child work with judging completeness by asking him or her to trace a picture of an object but to leave something out, such as a wagon without a wheel. Then your child should ask other family members if they can find out what's missing.

Can You Draw an Idea?
Help your child distinguish between concrete and abstract things by asking him or her to draw a picture of each of *dream*. Ask which are concrete things and which are abstract things. It will probably be much easier to draw a picture of the concrete things, because they can be seen, heard, felt, smelled, and tasted. Abstract things, such as *love, idea,* and *dream,* are not easy to picture.

Does This Make Sense?
Have fun with discussing logic of actions by asking your child to think of silly things to do, such as taking a bath on Main Street or swimming in syrup. After each suggestion, ask your child why each statement may not make sense.

Who, What, When, Where, How?
You can help your child understand the elements of a story by talking about a book he or she has recently read. Example questions are:

- Who are the main characters in the story?
- What happened in the story?
- When and where did the story take place?
- How did the story end?

Commercial Alert
You can help your child recognize fallacies in commercials. The next time you see or hear a commercial that makes certain claims, discuss with your child what the commercial is trying to convince you of. For example, will eating a certain cereal or wearing a certain shoe make

School-Home Newsletters for each unit include motivating At-Home activities that reinforce skills.

SCOPE & SEQUENCE

	Level A	Level B	Level C	Level D	Level E	Level F
UNIT 1 Knowing	**5**	**5**	**5**	**5**	**5**	**5**
Skill 1 Classifying	6–10	6–10	6–10	6–10	6–8	6–8
Skill 2 Real and Fanciful	11–14	11–14	11–12	11–12	9–10	9–10
Skill 3 Fact and Opinion	15–18	15–18	13–16	13–16	11–12	11–14
Skill 4 Definition and Example	19–22	19–22	17–20	17–20	13–14	15–16
Skill 5 Outlining and Summarizing	23–26	23–26	21–24	21–24	15–18	17–20
UNIT 2 Understanding	**29**	**29**	**27**	**27**	**21**	**23**
Skill 6 Comparing and Contrasting	30–32	30–32	28–30	28–30	22–24	24–26
Skill 7 Identifying Structure	33–34	33–34	31–32	31–32	25–26	27–28
Skill 8 Steps in a Process	35–38	35–38	33–34	33–34	27–28	29–30
Skill 9 Figural Relationships	39–40	39–40	35–36	35–36	29–30	31–32
Skill 10 Comparing Word Meanings	41–42	41–42	37–38	37–38	31–32	33–34
Skill 11 Identifying Main Ideas	43–46	43–46	39–42	39–42	33–34	35–36
Skill 12 Identifying Relationships	47–50	47–50	43–46	43–46	35–38	37–40
UNIT 3 Applying	**53**	**53**	**49**	**49**	**41**	**43**
Skill 13 Ordering Objects	54–56	54–56	50–52	50–52	42–44	44–46
Skill 14 Estimating	57–60	57–60	53–54	53–54	45–46	47–48
Skill 15 Anticipating Probabilities	61–64	61–64	55–58	55–58	47–48	49–50
Skill 16 Inferring	65–68	65–68	59–62	59–62	49–52	51–54
Skill 17 Changes in Word Meanings	69–70	69–72	63–66	63–64	53–56	55–56

	Level A	Level B	Level C	Level D	Level E	Level F
UNIT 4 Analyzing	**73**	**75**	**69**	**67**	**59**	**59**
Skill 18 Judging Completeness	74–76	76–78	70–72	68–70	60–62	60–62
Skill 19 Relevance of Information	77–80	79–80	73–74	71–72	63–64	63–64
Skill 20 Abstract or Concrete	81–84	81–84	75–76	73–74	65–66	65–66
Skill 21 Logic of Actions	85–88	85–88	77–78	75–76	67–68	67–68
Skill 22 Elements of a Selection	89–90	89–90	79–80	77–78	69–70	69–70
Skill 23 Story Logic	91–94	91–92	81–82	79–80	71–72	71–72
Skill 24 Recognizing Fallacies		93–94	83–86	81–84	73–76	73–76
UNIT 5 Synthesizing			**89**	**87**	**79**	**79**
Skill 25 Communicating Ideas			90–92	88–90	80–82	80–82
Skill 26 Planning Projects			93–94	91–94	83–86	83–86
Skill 27 Building Hypotheses			95–98	95–98	87–90	87–90
Skill 28 Drawing Conclusions			99–102	99–102	91–96	91–96
Skill 29 Proposing Alternatives			103–106	103–106	97–102	97–102
UNIT 6 Evaluating			**109**	**109**	**105**	**105**
Skill 30 Testing Generalizations			110–112	110–112	106–108	106–108
Skill 31 Developing Criteria			113–114	113–114	109–112	109–112
Skill 32 Judging Accuracy			115–118	115–118	113–116	113–116
Skill 33 Making Decisions			119–122	119–122	117–120	117–120
Skill 34 Identifying Values			123–124	123–124	121–124	121–124
Skill 35 Mood of a Story			125–126	125–126	125–126	125–126

CORRELATION TO CONTENT AREAS

	Level A	Level B	Level C	Level D	Level E	Level F
Reading and Language Arts	12, 13, 14, 15, 16, 17, 18, 22, 23, 26, 30, 34, 35, 36, 37, 41, 42, 43, 44, 45, 46, 51, 52, 55, 65, 66, 67, 68, 69, 70, 71, 72, 75, 79, 80, 83, 84, 88, 89, 90, 91, 92, 93, 94, 95, 96	7, 9, 11, 12, 13, 14, 15, 16, 17, 20, 21, 22, 24, 25, 27, 28, 32, 34, 35, 37, 41, 42, 43, 45, 46, 50, 52, 61, 62, 63, 65, 67, 68, 69, 70, 71, 72, 74, 78, 80, 82, 88, 89, 90, 91, 92, 94, 96	6, 11, 12, 13, 14, 15, 16, 25, 29, 30, 31, 32, 37, 38, 39, 40, 43, 44, 45, 46, 48, 55, 56, 57, 59, 60, 61, 62, 63, 64, 65, 66, 67, 68, 70, 72, 73, 74, 75, 77, 78, 79, 80, 81, 82, 83, 84, 85, 86, 87, 88, 93, 95, 96, 97, 98, 101, 102, 110, 112, 116, 117, 119, 120, 121, 122, 123, 124, 125, 126, 128	7, 11, 12, 13, 14, 15, 16, 19, 20, 21, 26, 30, 31, 32, 33, 36, 37, 38, 39, 40, 42, 44, 45, 48, 55, 56, 57, 58, 59, 61, 62, 63, 64, 65, 66, 67, 69, 70, 71, 73, 75, 76, 77, 78, 79, 80, 81, 82, 83, 84, 85, 88, 89, 95, 96, 97, 98, 99, 100, 104, 105, 106, 112, 113, 116, 117, 119, 120, 121, 123, 124, 125, 126, 128	9, 10, 11, 12, 13, 15, 16, 19, 23, 24, 25, 26, 27, 31, 32, 35, 37, 39, 42, 47, 48, 49, 50, 51, 52, 53, 54, 55, 56, 57, 58, 61, 65, 66, 67, 69, 70, 71, 73, 74, 75, 76, 77, 78, 80, 82, 83, 87, 88, 89, 90, 92, 93, 94, 97, 98, 99, 100, 102, 106, 107, 111, 112, 117, 120, 121, 122, 123, 125, 126, 128	6, 9, 11, 15, 16, 17, 18, 19, 20, 22, 25, 26, 27, 33, 34, 35, 36, 38, 39, 40, 42, 51, 52, 53, 55, 56, 58, 60, 62, 64, 66, 68, 70, 71, 73, 76, 78, 82, 88, 89, 95, 96, 102, 113, 115, 120, 123, 125, 126, 128
Social Studies	7, 8, 9, 10, 20, 25, 49, 54, 61, 76, 77, 78, 85, 87	6, 8, 10, 18, 23, 26, 31, 33, 38, 47, 48, 49, 64, 66, 77, 79, 81, 85, 86, 87, 90	7, 9, 10, 22, 23, 26, 28, 33, 35, 42, 47, 76, 90, 92, 100, 103, 104, 105, 106, 107, 108, 114, 115, 118, 127	6, 8, 9, 10, 24, 25, 28, 46, 50, 58, 72, 74, 86, 91, 92, 93, 101, 103, 115, 118, 122	7, 14, 15, 17, 28, 33, 36, 38, 44, 57, 60, 62, 63, 64, 68, 70, 81, 84, 85, 101, 113, 114, 116, 118, 119, 127	7, 12, 13, 14, 29, 30, 32, 35, 37, 41, 45, 50, 54, 57, 63, 65, 67, 69, 72, 74, 75, 83, 85, 90, 92, 97, 98, 99, 100, 101, 102, 108, 110, 112, 113, 114, 117, 118, 119, 121, 122, 123, 124
Science	6, 11, 19, 21, 24, 27, 28, 36, 38, 47, 48, 50, 62, 63, 64, 81, 86	19, 25, 44, 51, 64, 80, 93, 95	17, 18, 19, 20, 21, 23, 24, 34, 39, 41, 58, 90, 94, 99, 111, 113	17, 18, 22, 23, 29, 41, 43, 52, 90, 94, 107, 108, 110, 111, 114	6, 8, 18, 20, 22, 33, 34, 40, 72, 86, 91, 96, 103, 104, 108, 110, 115, 124	8, 10, 19, 24, 45, 46, 49, 61, 77, 80, 81, 84, 86, 87, 91, 93, 94, 98, 103, 106, 107, 116
Math	31, 32, 33, 39, 40, 54, 56, 57, 58, 59, 60, 74, 82	30, 36, 39, 40, 54, 55, 56, 57, 58, 59, 60, 73, 76, 83, 84	8, 36, 50, 51, 52, 53, 54, 71, 90, 91, 107	34, 35, 46, 47, 51, 53, 54, 60, 68, 90, 102, 109, 127	29, 30, 42, 43, 45, 46, 95, 109	21, 28, 31, 32, 44, 47, 48, 80, 94, 104, 109, 111, 120, 127

SKILL 1 PAGES 6–8 Classifying

STEP ONE Define the Skill

Discuss with your pupils the meaning of ***classifying:* grouping objects, people, or ideas because they are alike in some way.**

STEP TWO Identify the Steps

Explain to your pupils the steps they need to follow to classify any group of items, large or small:

1. Look at the items and decide which are similar in some way.
2. Place the similar items together in one group.
3. Assign a name to each group.
4. See if you can classify the items in one group into smaller groups.

STEP THREE Demonstrate the Skill

Ask pupils to watch and listen as you classify a group of items, following Step Two. **SUGGESTION:** Write the names of different kinds of sports on the board in random order. Then write four numbered categories—*Water Sports, Winter Sports, Field Sports, Court Sports.* Write each sport under the appropriate category name, explaining why you are grouping them this way. Show pupils that one category may also be divided into smaller categories or be part of a larger category—for example, *baseball and soccer are field sports played by teams, not individuals; these team field sports, along with most court sports, are ball games.*

STEP FOUR Practice the Skill

Use pages 6–8. See *Teacher Note* on each page.

STEP FIVE Provide Feedback

Discuss pupils' answers. **METACOGNITION:** Ask pupils to describe what they did. You may need to ask: **How did you decide to which group an item belonged? What did you look at or think about in making that decision?**

ENRICHMENT ACTIVITIES

Assemble objects, such as a book, a magazine, an encyclopedia, and a newspaper. Then have pupils establish criteria that would include most or all of the objects. For example, all are made from paper, and all are reading materials.

Provide a list of story titles and have pupils prepare a table of contents that arranges the stories into units. Possible story titles of "A Day at the Circus" and "The Art of Clowning" might be included in a unit entitled "Circus Fun."

Have pupils list criteria for choosing a good school. Then have them write an editorial explaining why each of their criteria is important to today's schools.

SKILL 2 PAGES 9–10 Real and Fanciful

STEP ONE Define the Skill

Discuss with your pupils the meaning of distinguishing between ***real and fanciful:* knowing the difference between things that exist and things that are only imagined.**

STEP TWO Identify the Steps

Explain to your pupils the steps they need to follow to know the difference between real and fanciful:

1. Read the text carefully.
2. Decide whether the text describes something that can exist or can happen, or something that can only be imagined.

STEP THREE Demonstrate the Skill

Ask pupils to watch and listen as you show the difference between real and fanciful, following Step Two. **SUGGESTION:** Write two sentences on the board—*I'm so hungry I could eat a quarter-pound burger,* and *I'm so hungry I could eat a horse.* Point out that the sentences are the same except for the final phrases. Explain that the first sentence describes what a hungry person could really eat; the second sentence does not. Therefore, the first statement could be real; the second is imaginary, or fanciful.

STEP FOUR Practice the Skill

Use pages 9–10. See *Teacher Note* on each page.

STEP FIVE Provide Feedback

Discuss pupils' answers. **METACOGNITION:** Ask pupils to describe what they did. You may need to ask: **How did you decide which statements were real and which were fanciful?**

ENRICHMENT ACTIVITIES

Read Native American or African folktales that explain something in nature, such as *How The Leopard Got Its Spots.* Then encourage pupils to write their own folktale about how a modern day reality came to be.

Ask pupils to write a paragraph explaining how they would help a preschool child distinguish between real and fanciful events.

Display words or phrases, such as *mysterious* and *creeping vines,* that could be used in either a fanciful story or a realistic story. Have pupils explain how they would use each word in different contexts.

SKILL 3 PAGES 11–12 Fact and Opinion

STEP ONE Define the Skill

Discuss with your pupils the meaning of telling the difference between ***fact and opinion:*** **knowing the difference between statements that can be proved true and statements that cannot be proved true.**

STEP TWO Identify the Steps

Explain to your pupils the steps they need to follow to know the difference between fact and opinion:

1. Read a statement and decide whether it could be proved true. If it can, it is a fact.
2. Look for words such as *feel, think, best,* and *wonderful* in a statement. They are clues that this statement gives an opinion.

STEP THREE Demonstrate the Skill

Ask pupils to watch and listen as you show the difference between fact and opinion, following Step Two. **SUGGESTION:** Write two sentences on the board—*Lake Superior is the largest of the Great Lakes,* and *Lake Superior is the prettiest of the Great Lakes.* Explain how the first statement can be proved true *(by looking it up in a reference book).* Explain how the second statement cannot be proved true. Point out that it also has a clue word signaling that it is an opinion *(prettiest).* Caution pupils that opinions do not always have clue words.

STEP FOUR Practice the Skill

Use pages 11–12. See *Teacher Note* on each page.

STEP FIVE Provide Feedback

Discuss pupils' answers. **METACOGNITION:** Ask pupils to describe what they did. You may need to ask: **How did you decide a statement was a fact? How could you prove the fact? How did you decide a statement was an opinion? Did any words give you a clue?**

ENRICHMENT ACTIVITIES

Ask volunteers to retell a favorite mystery story that they have read. Then talk about the distinction between eyewitness accounts and circumstantial evidence. Discuss which kind of evidence is more convincing and why.

Ask pupils whether a doctor or a friend is the more reliable source to discuss a medical problem with. Then have pupils work in groups to pose specific questions and possible sources of information. Discuss the reliability of suggested sources.

Choose a topic for a class newsletter. One group should write an editorial expressing an opinion about the topic. Each of three other groups should ask a factual question about the topic, collect data, and present findings in an article.

SKILL 4 PAGES 13–14 Definition and Example

STEP ONE Define the Skill

Discuss with your pupils the difference between ***definition and example:*** **the difference between giving the meaning of a word and naming things that belonged to the group described by the word.**

STEP TWO Identify the Steps

Explain to your pupils the steps they need to follow to know the difference between definitions and examples:

1. Read each sentence or phrase and ask: *Does it tell the meaning of a word?* If so, it is a definition.
2. Ask: *Does the sentence or phrase name things that belong to a group?* If so, it is an example.

STEP THREE Demonstrate the Skill

Ask pupils to watch and listen as you show the difference between a definition of a word and examples of the word, following Step Two. **SUGGESTION:** Write two sentences on the board—*A dog is a four-legged animal that is kept as a pet,* and *Dalmatians and Chihuahuas are two very different kinds of dogs.* Point out the part in the first sentence that defines the word *dog (is a four-legged animal that is kept as a pet).* Explain that the Chihuahuas and Dalmations named in the second sentence are examples of the group of animals called *dogs.*

STEP FOUR Practice the Skill

Use pages 13–14. See *Teacher Note* on each page.

STEP FIVE Provide Feedback

Discuss pupils' answers. **METACOGNITION:** Ask pupils to describe what they did. You may need to ask: **How could you tell when you were reading a definition? How could you tell when you were reading examples of a group?**

ENRICHMENT ACTIVITIES

Explain that a definition of an object *(torch)* can tell about its structure *(tool that uses fuel to produce a hot flame)* or describe how it functions *(used to melt metals, solder, or burn off paint).* Have pupils give the two types of definitions for *candle* or *glass.*

A concept can be explained by telling what is true about it and by telling what is *not* true about it. For example, a pond may be defined as, "a small body of water that is often shallow, calm, and quiet. It is not rough or large like an ocean."

Pupils may enjoy making up words and giving them definitions and examples. Challenge pupils to use their new words in oral sentences.

SKILL 5 PAGES 15–18 Outlining and Summarizing

STEP ONE Define the Skill

Discuss with your pupils the meaning of ***outlining and summarizing:*** **short ways of presenting information. When you outline, you list the main points and details in an organized way. When you summarize, you give only the main points.**

STEP TWO Identify the Steps

Explain to your pupils the steps they need to follow to summarize and outline:

1. Find the main idea—the most important idea in the paragraph or story.
2. Find the details—the information that explains the main idea.
3. To outline, number the main ideas with Roman numerals. List details under each main idea and mark them with capital letters.
4. To summarize, state the main idea in your own words. Leave out the details.

STEP THREE Demonstrate the Skill

Ask pupils to watch and listen as you outline and summarize, following Step Two. **SUGGESTION:** Select a story pupils have just read in their reading books. Summarize the story with a statement of the main idea. Then outline the story on the board, explaining how to mark main ideas and details with Roman numerals and capital letters.

STEP FOUR Practice the Skill

Use pages 15–18. See *Teacher Note* on each page.

STEP FIVE Provide Feedback

Discuss pupils' answers. **METACOGNITION:** Ask pupils to describe what they did. You may need to ask: **How did you decide which statement best summarized the main idea? How did you choose the facts that help support the main ideas? How did you know whether to put an idea after a Roman numeral or a capital letter in the outline?**

ENRICHMENT ACTIVITIES

Provide pupils with a topic under which a series of related details may be organized. You may use a topic in science which pupils have studied, such as *The Water Cycle.* Ask pupils to outline the related details.

Provide pupils with a set of notes about a flood, such as those a newspaper reporter might jot down at the scene. Ask pupils to use the notes to write a news article summarizing the event.

Have pupils write a brief outline of their life. They should begin with headings, such as *family, school, interests, future plans,* and then add details to each heading in the outline.

UNIT 2

Understanding

BLOOM'S TAXONOMY

KNOWLEDGE	COMPREHENSION	APPLICATION	ANALYSIS	SYNTHESIS	EVALUATION

UNIT 2: UNDERSTANDING PAGES

COMPREHENSION is the term used in Bloom's Taxonomy for the second stage in cognitive development. Comprehension refers to the basic level of understanding and involves the ability to know what is being communicated in order to make use of the information. This includes translating or interpreting a communication or extrapolating information from a communication.

The authors of this program have identified the following skills as being particularly helpful in developing Bloom's second stage:

1. Comparing and Contrasting
2. Identifying Structure
3. Identifying Steps in a Process
4. Understanding Figural Relationships
5. Comparing Word Meanings
6. Identifying Main Ideas
7. Identifying Relationships

Step-by-step procedures for teaching each of these skills follow. These lesson plans will help you use the program with ease as you incorporate ***thinking skills*** into your teaching day. Enrichment activities that accompany each lesson will help your students apply their newly acquired thinking skills to a variety of situations.

After this unit has been completed, copy and distribute the School-Home Newsletter on page T-43.

SKILL 6 PAGES 22–24 Comparing and Contrasting

STEP ONE Define the Skill

Discuss with your pupils the meaning of ***comparing and contrasting:*** **examining things to see their similarities and differences.**

STEP TWO Identify the Steps

Explain to your pupils the steps they need to follow to compare and contrast two or more items:

1. Look carefully to see how the items are similar.
2. Look carefully to see how the items are different.

STEP THREE Demonstrate the Skill

Ask pupils to watch and listen as you compare and contrast a group of items, following Step Two. **SUGGESTION:** Present a list of plants—*maple tree, pine tree, rosebush, ivy, tulip plant*. Point out how they are all alike as members of a group—for example, *they are all plants, they all have green parts, and they all grow*. Point out the similarities between certain plants. For example, *maple trees and pine trees have woody trunks; rosebushes and tulip plants produce colorful flowers*. Then point out the differences—for example, *the maple tree loses its leaves each autumn, while the pine tree keeps its green needles; a tulip plant grows straight up from the ground, while ivy grows along the ground or up walls and fences; the rosebush has flower buds, while the pine tree produces cones.*

STEP FOUR Practice the Skill

Use pages 22–24. See *Teacher Note* on each page.

STEP FIVE Provide Feedback

Discuss pupils' answers. **METACOGNITION:** Ask pupils to describe what they did. You may need to ask: **What did you look at to find similarities and differences?**

ENRICHMENT ACTIVITIES

Provide pupils with editorials written about controversial issues. Help them compare and contrast the facts and opinions presented in each editorial.

Challenge pupils to compare items according to cost. They might arrange items, such as the following, from least expensive to most expensive: *car, brush, dictionary, bike,* and *telephone.*

Provide sentences that compare objects and challenge pupils to add a sentence that contrasts them. For example: *Jose's ten-speed bicycle is the same size and color as Ana's bicycle.* Pupils might add: *However, Jose's bicycle is a new model.*

SKILL 7 PAGES 25–26 Identifying Structure

STEP ONE Define the Skill

Discuss with your pupils the meaning of ***identifying structure:*** **finding out and describing how the parts of something are arranged and how they fit together to make up the whole.**

STEP TWO Identify the Steps

Explain to your pupils the steps they need to follow to identify the structure of something:

1. Look at the whole thing and tell what it is.
2. Look at the parts and list them.
3. See how the parts are arranged.
4. See how the parts together make up the whole.

STEP THREE Demonstrate the Skill

Ask pupils to watch and listen as you identify the structure of something, following Step Two. **SUGGESTION:** Write a limerick on the board, such as the following by an unknown author—*There was a young lady of Crete,/Who was so exceedingly neat,/When she got out of bed/She stood on her head,/To make sure of not soiling her feet.* Explain how a limerick is constructed of five lines. The first, second, and fifth lines always rhyme with one another. The third and fourth lines are shorter than the others and always rhyme with each other. Explain that the number of lines and the rhyme structure together help make up the limerick.

STEP FOUR Practice the Skill

Use pages 25–26. See *Teacher Note* on each page.

STEP FIVE Provide Feedback

Discuss pupils' answers. **METACOGNITION:** Ask pupils to describe what they did. You may need to ask: **How did you identify the parts of a whole? How did you study their arrangement?**

ENRICHMENT ACTIVITIES

Help pupils recognize that letters follow a structural format. Provide a sample business letter and a personal letter. Have pupils compare the two letters to see how they are alike. Have pupils discuss why the two kinds of letters have slightly different structures.

Challenge pupils to design an outdoor playground set that is strong, safe, and stable. Point out that stability comes from having several strong legs for support.

Challenge pupils to point out or describe unusual structures within your community. Encourage students to give their opinion on the beauty and usefulness of each structure.

SKILL 8 PAGES 27–28 Steps in a Process

STEP ONE Define the Skill

Discuss with your pupils the meaning of identifying ***steps in a process:* knowing the series of actions that lead to a particular result and figuring out what comes next in the series.**

STEP TWO Identify the Steps

Explain to your pupils the steps they need to follow to identify steps in a process:

1. Identify the result (the end, purpose, or goal) of the process.
2. Decide which steps are first and last.
3. Figure out the order of the remaining steps.
4. Check whether any steps are missing.

STEP THREE Demonstrate the Skill

Ask pupils to watch and listen as you identify the steps in a process, following Step Two. **SUGGESTION:** List in random order the actions needed to get a library book—for example, *give library card to librarian, look at guide numbers on shelves, check card catalog for the number of the book, check numbers of books along shelf, take book to checkout counter, locate book.* State the purpose or end result of the process—*a checked-out library book.* Decide which steps are first and last. Number the remaining steps in order. Check to see whether any steps have been left out.

STEP FOUR Practice the Skill

Use pages 27–28. See *Teacher Note* on each page.

STEP FIVE Provide Feedback

Discuss pupils' answers. **METACOGNITION:** Ask pupils to describe what they did. You may need to ask: **How did you know which steps came first and which came last? How did you decide the order of the rest of the steps?**

ENRICHMENT ACTIVITIES

Ask pupils to interview a working adult about his or her job. Direct pupils to ask the interviewee to teach them one process the adult must repeat regularly in his or her job. Then have pupils write about the steps that person must take to do the job.

Pupils might enjoy researching and writing about the steps involved in an election. Guide students to begin with a candidate's decision to run for the office and end with the actual election.

Ask pupils to think about a favorite activity or hobby. Challenge them to outline the steps necessary to learn it. Then have pupils list the steps for someone who may be interested in learning more about the hobby or activity.

SKILL 9 PAGES 29–30 Figural Relationships

STEP ONE Define the Skill

Discuss with your pupils the meaning of understanding ***figural relationships:*** **using figures to get information and see connections between ideas.**

STEP TWO Identify the Steps

Explain to your pupils the steps they need to follow when using figures to get information and see connections:

1. Look at the whole figure to see what main information it gives.
2. Look at the parts of the figure to see the specific information they give you.
3. See how one part of the figure is related to another part.

STEP THREE Demonstrate the Skill

Ask pupils to watch and listen as you use a figure to get information, following Step Two. **SUGGESTION:** Draw a simple pie graph on the board. The whole circle represents the total number of pupils in your class. Divide the circle into sections to show the percentage of girls and the percentage of boys in the class. Explain that the whole figure is showing the size of the class; each section shows the size of a subgroup. The figure allows you to see which group, if either, is larger.

STEP FOUR Practice the Skill

Use pages 29–30. See *Teacher Note* on each page.

STEP FIVE Provide Feedback

Discuss pupils' answers. **METACOGNITION:** Ask pupils to describe what they did. You may need to ask: **How did you locate the individual parts, or facts, in the figure? How did you decide on the total meaning of the figure?**

ENRICHMENT ACTIVITIES

Display and identify flags that have symbols on them. Discuss the meaning of each symbol, helping pupils see that symbols are used to convey an idea. Then ask students to design a flag for their city or town. Encourage pupils to explain why they chose the symbols they used.

Have pupils locate and interpret graphs in newspapers or magazines. Challenge them to research data about their school. Then have pupils make their own graph for a class display.

Have pupils illustrate the structure of an imaginary solar system. Then have pairs of pupils compare their illustrations to find similarities and differences.

SKILL 10 PAGES 31–32 Comparing Word Meanings

STEP ONE Define the Skill

Discuss with your pupils the meaning of ***comparing word meanings:*** **getting to know words whose meanings are similar, different, or changed by spelling or pronunciation.**

STEP TWO Identify the Steps

Explain to your pupils the steps they need to follow to compare word meanings:

1. Look at the word and pronounce it.
2. Decide what the word means.
3. Think of synonyms.
4. Think of antonyms.
5. See if you can add or drop letters to make a new word. See how this change also changes the meaning.

STEP THREE Demonstrate the Skill

Ask pupils to watch and listen as you compare word meanings, following Step Two. **SUGGESTION:** Show how much information the dictionary gives about word meanings by looking up the word *short.* Pronounce the word and read the meanings. Read or suggest synonyms and antonyms. Add letters to create new words and meanings—*shortening, shortstop*—and read those definitions from the dictionary.

STEP FOUR Practice the Skill

Use pages 31–32. See *Teacher Note* on each page.

STEP FIVE Provide Feedback

Discuss pupils' answers. **METACOGNITION:** Ask pupils to describe what they did. You may need to ask: **How did you choose words that were related? How did you choose synonyms?**

ENRICHMENT ACTIVITIES

Have pupils work in groups to write sentences that contain antonyms. For example: *The living room looked* old, *but the kitchen was very* modern. *She moved slowly out of the* darkness *and into the* light.

Make a word web for the word *hard*. Add words that are synonyms of *hard*, such as *difficult*, *strong*, and *cold-hearted*. Then extend the web to include synonyms for each word of the first list synonyms.

Have pupils illustrate two imaginary extraterrestrials that are opposite in looks. Encourage pupils to be creative and allow pupils to work together if they wish.

SKILL 11 PAGES 33–34 Identifying Main Ideas

STEP ONE Define the Skill

Discuss with your pupils the meaning of ***identifying main ideas:*** **knowing the major point in written material or in a picture and noting how certain details tell about the major point.**

STEP TWO Identify the Steps

Explain to your pupils the steps they need to follow to identify main ideas:

1. Read the section or study the picture.
2. Decide what the major point is.
3. Find the major idea in a sentence or state it in your own words.
4. Note which details help support the main idea.

STEP THREE Demonstrate the Skill

Ask pupils to watch and listen as you identify the main idea of a paragraph, following Step Two. **SUGGESTION:** Write this paragraph on the board—*Everybody has a strong point—something he or she can do well. Some people are smart in school. Others are good at sports, music, or art. Some people make friends easily. Still others have a hobby at which they excel.* Read the paragraph. Note that people's strong points are the topic. Find the sentence with the main idea—the first sentence. Note how the details in the other sentences tell about that point. Erase the first sentence and show how you can also tell the main idea just by reading the sentences with details.

STEP FOUR Practice the Skill

Use pages 33–34. See *Teacher Note* on each page.

STEP FIVE Provide Feedback

Discuss pupils' answers. **METACOGNITION:** Ask pupils to describe what they did. You may need to ask: **How did you choose the sentence that told the main idea? How did you write your own topic sentence?**

ENRICHMENT ACTIVITIES

Have pupils write a paragraph that begins with a statement of the main idea and then rewrite the paragraph with the statement of the main idea last. Compare the effectiveness of each paragraph.

Read several paragraphs, leaving out the statement of the main idea. Challenge pupils to provide a main-idea sentence for each paragraph. Then have pupils write similar paragraphs for a partner to guess the main idea.

Ask each pupil to write a paragraph that includes extraneous information that does not support the main idea of the paragraph. Then allow them to exchange papers and have a partner find the extraneous information.

Identifying Relationships

STEP ONE Define the Skill

Discuss with your pupils the meaning of ***identifying relationships:*** **seeing the connection between two or more objects, events, or ideas.**

STEP TWO Identify the Steps

Explain to your pupils the steps they need to follow to identify relationships:

1. Read carefully. Think about the objects, events, or ideas you are reading about.
2. Ask yourself how these things are related. Does one thing happen before or after another? Does one thing cause another? Does one thing happen near another?

STEP THREE Demonstrate the Skill

Ask pupils to watch and listen as you identify relationships, following Step Two. **SUGGESTION:** Write examples of Roman numerals on the board—for example, *I, IV, VI, XX, XXI, XXIX*. Note how each figure has a value of its own, but its spatial relationship to other figures determines the overall value of the numeral (*I before V means 5 – 1, but I after V means 5 + 1,* and so on).

STEP FOUR Practice the Skill

Use pages 35–38. See *Teacher Note* on each page.

STEP FIVE Provide Feedback

Discuss pupils' answers. **METACOGNITION:** Ask pupils to describe what they did. You may need to ask: **What did you think about to relate objects, events, or ideas in your mind?**

ENRICHMENT ACTIVITIES

Have pupils find cause-and-effect relationships in a reading selection. Challenge pupils to describe an effect from their selection and ask the class to guess what the cause might have been.

Offer situations and have pupils identify a likely result of a cause. For example: An automobile plant closed and laid off workers. What results might reasonably be expected?

Have pupils list a few actions they have taken in the past few days and allow them to explain why they did them.

UNIT 3

Applying

BLOOM'S TAXONOMY

KNOWLEDGE	COMPREHENSION	APPLICATION	ANALYSIS	SYNTHESIS	EVALUATION

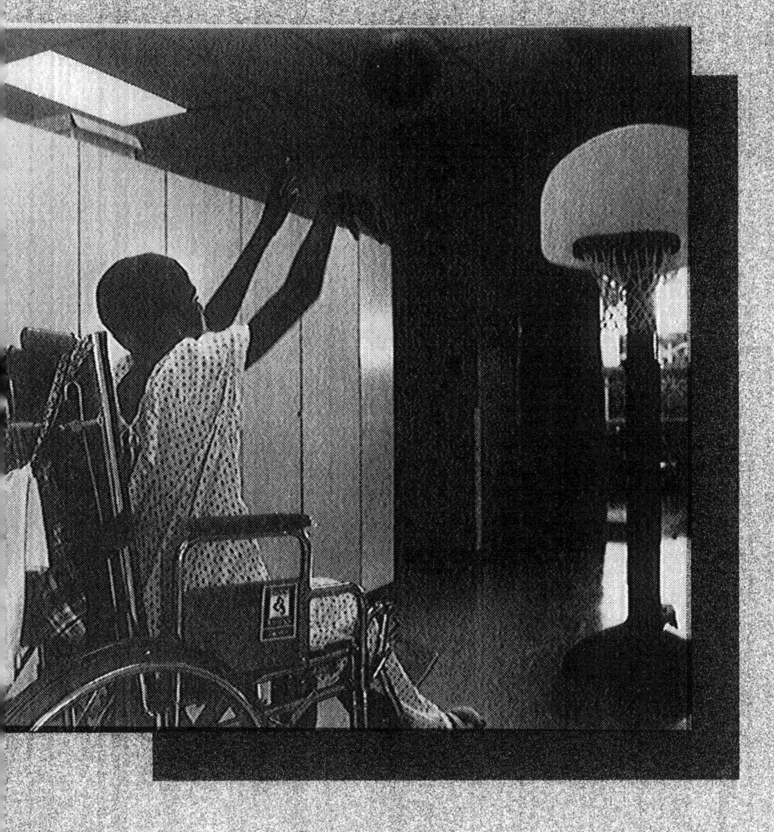

APPLICATION is the term used in Bloom's Taxonomy for the third stage in cognitive development. Application is the ability to use a learned skill in a new situation.

The authors of this program have identified the following skills as being particularly helpful in developing Bloom's third stage:

1. Ordering Objects
2. Estimating
3. Anticipating Probabilities
4. Inferring
5. Interpreting Changes in Word Meanings

Step-by-step procedures for teaching each of these skills follow. These lesson plans will help you use the program with ease as you incorporate ***thinking skills*** into your teaching day. Enrichment activities that accompany each lesson will help your students apply their newly acquired thinking skills to a variety of situations.

After this unit has been completed, copy and distribute the School-Home Newsletter on page T-44.

SKILL 13 PAGES 42–44 — Ordering Objects

STEP ONE Define the Skill
Discuss with your pupils the meaning of *ordering objects:* **putting items in order according to a pattern.**

STEP TWO Identify the Steps
Explain to your pupils the steps they need to follow to order objects:
1. Skim the items.
2. Identify the pattern that should determine the order of the items.
3. Decide which object is first and which is last.
4. Put the remaining objects in order between the first and last.

STEP THREE Demonstrate the Skill
Ask pupils to watch and listen as you order a group of objects, following Step Two. **SUGGESTION:** List the following animals on the board—*centipede, stork, spider, millipede, ant, horse.* Tell pupils that you will order the animals according to the number of legs they have—from fewest to greatest. Identify the fewest—*stork*—and the greatest—*millipede.* Then place the remaining animals in order—*horse, ant, spider, centipede.*

STEP FOUR Practice the Skill
Use pages 42–44. See *Teacher Note* on each page.

STEP FIVE Provide Feedback
Discuss pupils' answers. **METACOGNITION:** Ask pupils to describe what they did. You may need to ask: **How did you decide which item came first? Which came last? How did you decide the order of the remaining items?**

ENRICHMENT ACTIVITIES

List five or six animal names in order by size or list historic events in chronological order. Then have pupils add their own examples to the list.

Pupils may enjoy listing ten movies they have seen and then ordering them from their most favorite to their least favorite.

Have pupils write their name and birthday on the board. Then have the class order the names chronologically to follow the school year.

SKILL 14 PAGES 45–46 — Estimating

STEP ONE Define the Skill
Discuss with your pupils the meaning of *estimating:* **using facts to make an educated guess.**

STEP TWO Identify the Steps
Explain to your pupils the steps they need to follow to estimate:
1. Picture in your mind the size, time, or amount of the things you are estimating.
2. Look for other facts you may need in order to estimate.
3. Use the picture in your mind and the facts to make a good guess.

STEP THREE Demonstrate the Skill
Ask pupils to watch and listen as you estimate, following Step Two. **SUGGESTION:** Hold a picture of a crowd of people in front of pupils. Count the number of people in a small group in one corner of the picture. Then estimate how many people are in the entire crowd. Explain to pupils that you visualize that same size group of people side by side, covering the entire picture, then multiply the number of groups you visualized by the number of people in the group you actually counted. Emphasize the importance of imagining—or visualizing—when estimating.

STEP FOUR Practice the Skill
Use pages 45–46. See *Teacher Note* on each page.

STEP FIVE Provide Feedback
Discuss pupils' answers. **METACOGNITION:** Ask pupils to describe what they did. You may need to ask: **Could you picture what you were estimating? What else did you look at or think about to come up with a good estimate?**

ENRICHMENT ACTIVITIES

Challenge pupils to name situations in everyday life in which estimating is needed.

Have pupils estimate how many pupils in all were absent last week. Then with the class, tally the actual number of pupils who have been absent from school in the past week.

Have pupils count the number of steps it takes to walk around the classroom. Then ask them to estimate how many steps it would take for them to walk around the school. Allow pupils to test their estimates.

SKILL 15 PAGES 47–48 Anticipating Probabilities

STEP ONE Define the Skill

Discuss with your pupils the meaning of ***anticipating probabilities:*** **predicting what is likely to occur next.**

STEP TWO Identify the Steps

Explain to your pupils the steps they need to follow to anticipate probabilities:

1. Note all the facts that are given.
2. Think of events that might happen as a result.
3. Predict which event is most likely to happen.

STEP THREE Demonstrate the Skill

Ask pupils to watch and listen as you anticipate probabilities, following Step Two. **SUGGESTION:** Present a situation to pupils—for example, *It's a hot, humid summer day, and you are on your way to your uncle's ice cream store.* Think of what effect the weather might have on the store's business. Predict which thing is most likely to happen—*The store will likely be much busier than usual.*

STEP FOUR Practice the Skill

Use pages 47–48. See *Teacher Note* on each page.

STEP FIVE Provide Feedback

Discuss pupils' answers. **METACOGNITION:** Ask pupils to describe what they did. You may need to ask: **How did you decide what would probably happen? How did you choose whether something was probable or just possible?**

ENRICHMENT ACTIVITIES

Present situations to pupils and ask them to write their own endings. For example: *As the car door slammed, Joyce cried out, "Oh, my finger;" As John stepped on the beach, the sand burned his feet.*

Write the names of several vegetables on the board. Have pupils use their own experience to predict which vegetables the class likes best. Then have pupils rank the vegetables in their order of preference. Compare individual rankings to determine how the majority of pupils ranked them.

Tell pupils to imagine that it is fifty years ago. Ask them to write about how they think their life might be different if they were to go back to that time.

SKILL 16 PAGES 49–52 Inferring

STEP ONE Define the Skill

Discuss with your pupils the meaning of ***inferring:*** **using information that is stated to come up with other information that is not directly stated but seems likely to be true from what you know.**

STEP TWO Identify the Steps

Explain to your pupils the steps they need to follow to infer:

1. Note carefully all the pieces of information you are given.
2. Think of what else must be true, using the information.

STEP THREE Demonstrate the Skill

Ask pupils to watch and listen as you infer, following Step Two. **SUGGESTION:** Read the following paragraph aloud—*Juan was racing down the sidewalk toward the school bus stop. If he missed the bus, he would be late for the third time this week. Anxiously, he turned the corner. There before him stood a familiar bunch of kids at the bus stop.* Note for pupils the information given—*the children still waiting at the bus stop.* Because they are "familiar" to Juan, you can infer that they are the children with whom he normally waits for the bus. And because they are still at the bus stop, you can infer that the bus has not yet come.

STEP FOUR Practice the Skill

Use pages 49–52. See *Teacher Note* on each page.

STEP FIVE Provide Feedback

Discuss pupils' answers. **METACOGNITION:** Ask pupils to describe what they did. You may need to ask: **What information did you use to infer your answer?**

ENRICHMENT ACTIVITIES

Provide a series of paragraphs that provides a character sketch. Have pupils infer from the context of the paragraphs the nature of the character. For example, is the character honest or deceitful?

Have pupils describe the uniforms athletes wear for each of three specific sports. Then challenge pupils to explain the reasoning behind each uniform design.

Explain that sometimes weather patterns move from west to east. Point to a place on the western part of a map and say there is a cloud cover there. Then point to a place east of the spot and ask pupils what they might infer.

SKILL 17 PAGES 53–56 Changes in Word Meanings

STEP ONE Define the Skill

Discuss with your pupils the meaning of interpreting ***changes in word meanings:*** **recognizing that a word can have different meanings depending on how it is used.**

STEP TWO Identify the Steps

Explain to your pupils the steps they need to follow to interpret changes in word meaning:

1. Look at the word. See if you can separate the word into meaningful parts—a prefix, a suffix, a root, two individual words.
2. Think of the most familiar meaning of the word.
3. Decide whether the familiar meaning is being used in this context.
4. If it is not, try to figure out the meaning based on the way the word is being used in this context.

STEP THREE Demonstrate the Skill

Ask pupils to watch and listen as you interpret changes in word meanings, following Step Two. **SUGGESTION:** Write a sentence on the board—for example, *If you can't bear to see a bear captive in a zoo, bear in mind that this creature could easily bear you off into the woods.* Note that the word *bear* is used four different times in the sentence with four different meanings. Use the context to determine the meaning in each case.

STEP FOUR Practice the Skill

Use pages 53–56. See *Teacher Note* on each page.

STEP FIVE Provide Feedback

Discuss pupils' answers. **METACOGNITION:** Ask pupils to describe what they did. You may need to ask: **Which sentence clues did you use to figure out the meaning of the word?**

ENRICHMENT ACTIVITIES

Discuss with pupils the meaning of certain idiomatic expressions, such as *give me a hand* and *wake up on time.* Challenge pairs of pupils to work together to compile a list of idiomatic expressions.

Have pupils add suffixes to root words you have written on the board. Discuss how the meaning changes as each suffix is added. Possibilities include: *hard—harder, hardest, hardly; help—helper, helpful, helpless.*

Have pupils write and illustrate a sentence that uses more than one meaning of a multiple-meaning word. The sentences may be real or fanciful. For example: *The pitcher pours a drink from a pitcher; A school of salmon went to school.*

UNIT 4

Analyzing

BLOOM'S TAXONOMY

KNOWLEDGE	COMPREHENSION	APPLICATION	ANALYSIS	SYNTHESIS	EVALUATION

UNIT 4: ANALYZING

ANALYSIS is the term used in Bloom's Taxonomy for the fourth stage in cognitive development. Analysis is the ability to break down information into its integral parts and to identify the relationship of each part to the total organization.

The authors of this program have identified the following skills as being particularly helpful in developing Bloom's fourth stage:

1. Judging Completeness
2. Judging Relevance of Information
3. Judging Abstract or Concrete
4. Judging Logic of Actions
5. Identifying Elements of a Selection
6. Judging Story Logic
7. Recognizing Fallacies

Step-by-step procedures for teaching each of these skills follow. These lesson plans will help you use the program with ease as you incorporate ***thinking skills*** into your teaching day. Enrichment activities that accompany each lesson will help your students apply their newly acquired thinking skills to a variety of situations.

After this unit has been completed, copy and distribute the School-Home Newsletter on page T-45.

SKILL 18 PAGES 60–62 Judging Completeness

STEP ONE Define the Skill

Discuss with your pupils the meaning of ***judging completeness:*** **determining whether information is missing from a picture, chart, or text.**

STEP TWO Identify the Steps

Explain to your pupils the steps they need to follow to judge completeness:

1. Look at the picture, or carefully read the text or chart.
2. Ask yourself if the information makes sense or if something is missing.
3. If you can, complete the item by providing the missing parts.

STEP THREE Demonstrate the Skill

Ask pupils to watch and listen as you judge the completeness of an item, following Step Two. **SUGGESTION**: Present the following word problem—*At the store you want to buy a magazine for $1.00, a set of colored markers for $2.50, and a postcard for each of your friends at $0.50 each. If you have a $5.00 bill with you, do you have enough money?* Point out that one necessary piece of information is missing—*the number of postcards you want to buy.* The information you need to solve the word problem is therefore incomplete.

STEP FOUR Practice the Skill

Use pages 60–62 See *Teacher Note* on each page.

STEP FIVE Provide Feedback

Discuss pupils' answers. **METACOGNITION:** Ask pupils to describe what they did. You may need to ask: **How could you tell when an item was incomplete? How did you decide what was needed to complete an item?**

ENRICHMENT ACTIVITIES

Pupils may enjoy asking several classmates for directions to a familiar location and then judging whose directions are most complete.

Provide each pupil with a simple drawing and have pupils write a story to give the details about the pictured event.

Challenge pupils to evaluate the completeness of their own homework and of tasks they perform at home. Was there more they could have done?

SKILL 19 PAGES 63–64 Relevance of Information

STEP ONE Define the Skill

Discuss with your pupils the meaning of judging ***relevance of information:*** **determining whether an idea or fact relates to a topic or is unneeded information.**

STEP TWO Identify the Steps

Explain to your pupils the steps they need to follow to judge relevance of information:

1. Identify the topic or task.
2. Think about the information you have.
3. Decide whether each fact helps to define or describe the topic or task.

STEP THREE Demonstrate the Skill

Ask pupils to watch and listen as you judge relevance of information, following Step Two. **SUGGESTION:** Present a situation to pupils—*You are given directions to a classmate's home from school. Your classmate tells you the names of streets you need to take, the number of blocks to walk on each street, which way to turn at corners, the address of her house, and how long her family has lived there.* Point out that one piece of information is not relevant—*how long her family has lived in the house*—because you don't need to know that in order to find her home.

STEP FOUR Practice the Skill

Use pages 63–64. See *Teacher Note* on each page.

STEP FIVE Provide Feedback

Discuss pupils' answers. **METACOGNITION:** Ask pupils to describe what they did. You may need to ask: **How did you decide which information you needed? How did you decide which information would be unnecessary?**

ENRICHMENT ACTIVITIES

Help pupils determine where they might find relevant information on such topics as learning to sail a boat.

Ask pupils to describe the information they would need to build a birdhouse. For example: *size of house needed for type of bird, size of hole, height of hole from floor, height of birdhouse from ground.*

Challenge pupils to find a newspaper article about a reported crime and to rewrite it as a police report, including only relevant information.

SKILL 20 PAGES 65–66 Abstract or Concrete

STEP ONE Define the Skill

Discuss with your pupils the meaning of deciding between ***abstract or concrete:*** **distinguishing between a term that refers to a general, intangible group and a term that refers to a specific member of the group.**

STEP TWO Identify the Steps

Explain to your pupils the steps they need to follow to distinguish between abstract or concrete:

1. Read the information.
2. Place terms that are referring to a large, general group in the abstract category.
3. Place terms that are referring to specific members of a group in the concrete category.

STEP THREE Demonstrate the Skill

Ask pupils to watch and listen as you show how to decide whether a term is abstract or concrete, following Step Two. **SUGGESTION:** Write the heading *Abstract* on the board. To its right, write the heading *Concrete.* Draw an arrow from *Abstract* to *Concrete.* Then write the following terms in order, placing the first under *Abstract,* the last under *Concrete,* and the middle two in between: *people, children, boys, Charles.* Explain that as you move from left to right, or from abstract to concrete, the terms become more and more specific.

STEP FOUR Practice the Skill

Use pages 65–66. See *Teacher Note* on each page.

STEP FIVE Provide Feedback

Discuss pupils' answers. **METACOGNITION:** Ask pupils to describe what they did. You may need to ask: **How did you decide whether something was abstract? How did you decide whether something was concrete?**

ENRICHMENT ACTIVITIES

Challenge pupils to design a personal coat of arms. Each of the four sections should have a drawing that represents the pupil's ideals or goals. For example, if the pupil loves to read, there might be a book pictured in one of the sections.

Ask pupils to write three short paragraphs—one about the actions of someone who is kind and gentle, one about someone who is impatient and irritable, and one about someone who is friendly and generous.

Present pupils with notes on a newsworthy event. Challenge them to write a newspaper article that gives concrete information.

SKILL 21 PAGES 67–68 Logic of Actions

STEP ONE Define the Skill

Discuss with your pupils the meaning of judging the *logic of actions:* **determining whether an action makes sense.**

STEP TWO Identify the Steps

Explain to your pupils the steps they need to follow to judge the logic of actions:

1. Study the situation.
2. Brainstorm several actions you could take in that situation.
3. Consider each action and its possible outcome.
4. Choose the action or actions that best fit the situation and the desired outcome.

STEP THREE Demonstrate the Skill

Ask pupils to watch and listen as you judge the logic of actions, following Step Two. **SUGGESTION:** Present a situation to the class—*Your parents have said you must share morning and evening dishwashing duties with your older sister. You start school a half hour later than your sister, and after dinner you have band practice.* List possible courses of action—*sharing the duty both morning and night; alternating days, or one washing dishes in the morning and the other washing them at night.* Explain how the one action that best fits the situation is for you to take morning dishwashing and your sister to wash them at night.

STEP FOUR Practice the Skill

Use pages 67–68. See *Teacher Note* on each page.

STEP FIVE Provide Feedback

Discuss pupils' answers. **METACOGNITION:** Ask pupils to describe what they did. You may need to ask: **How did you decide which action (or solution) made sense in each situation?**

ENRICHMENT ACTIVITIES

Choose a story everyone has read. Discuss the actions of several of the characters. Decide whether it made sense for the characters to act as they did.

Present a problem and have pupils brainstorm ways of solving it. Then have each pupil decide which is the best course of action and write a paragraph explaining his or her decision.

Have pupils keep a log of their actions for a day. Then have them write their comments about the appropriateness of their actions.

SKILL 22 PAGES 69–70 Elements of a Selection

STEP ONE Define the Skill

Discuss with your pupils the meaning of identifying the *elements of a selection:* **identifying the parts of a story—the characters, setting, and the plot.**

STEP TWO Identify the Steps

Explain to your pupils the steps they need to follow to identify the elements of a selection:

1. Read the story.
2. Find the main characters—the people or animals the story is about.
3. Note the setting—where and when the story takes place.
4. Describe the plot—the action that takes place.

STEP THREE Demonstrate the Skill

Ask pupils to watch and listen as you identify the elements of a selection, following Step Two. **SUGGESTION:** Select a previously read story, such as *My Side of the Mountain.* Name the main character *(Sam Gribley),* note where the setting or settings are *(the mountains),* and summarize the plot of the story *(surviving in the wilderness).*

STEP FOUR Practice the Skill

Use pages 69–70. See *Teacher Note* on each page.

STEP FIVE Provide Feedback

Discuss pupils' answers. **METACOGNITION:** Ask pupils to describe what they did. You may need to ask: **How did you identify the main characters? What parts helped you know where and when the story took place? How did you follow along with the action of the story?**

ENRICHMENT ACTIVITIES

Have the class brainstorm problems that a story character might face. Then choose and write a class story that provides a solution.

For a particular selection, have pupils rank the setting, characters, plot, author's purpose, theme, and style according to its importance to the story. Then have pupils analyze other selections in a similar manner.

Have pupils rewrite a familiar selection, such as *Sarah, Plain and Tall,* as though Sarah were telling the story from her perspective.

SKILL 23 PAGES 71–72 Story Logic

STEP ONE Define the Skill

Discuss with your pupils the meaning of judging *story logic:* **determining whether details and events in a story are related to the plot and whether they follow a logical order.**

STEP TWO Identify the Steps

Explain to your pupils the steps they need to follow to judge the logic of a story:

1. Determine the plot of the story.
2. Ask yourself whether each detail or event helps move the action forward or does not belong.
3. Make sure the events are in the right order.

STEP THREE Demonstrate the Skill

Ask pupils to watch and listen as you judge the logic of a short paragraph, following Step Two. SUGGESTION: Write the following paragraph on the board—*Melissa sold enough flower seeds to raise $65. Melissa was selling seeds to help raise money for her scout troop to go to camp. Melissa's mom is allergic to flowers. She sold seeds near the bank. Then she moved across the street to sell them near a flower store.* Explain that the main idea is Melissa's success at selling seeds. The first sentence should come last; it tells how successful Melissa was. The third sentence should be dropped; it doesn't belong because it doesn't have anything to do with Melissa's sales. Rewrite the paragraph correctly.

STEP FOUR Practice the Skill

Use pages 71–72. See *Teacher Note* on each page.

STEP FIVE Provide Feedback

Discuss pupils' answers. **METACOGNITION:** Ask pupils to describe what they did. You may need to ask: **What clues did you use to figure out the correct order of the events? How did you decide where each idea fit logically?**

ENRICHMENT ACTIVITIES

Discuss a story that the class has read and have them debate whether the actions of the main character made sense.

Explain that biographies usually are written chronologically. Have pupils choose a biography to read and then make a time line showing the sequence of main events in that person's life.

Have pupils write a story that includes the following events in order: *followed the footprints, heard a noise, saw raccoons eating food, noticed a bag of food was missing, saw footprints.*

Recognizing Fallacies

STEP ONE Define the Skill

Discuss with your pupils the meaning of ***recognizing fallacies:*** **recognizing statements that are based on false or bad reasoning.**

STEP TWO Identify the Steps

Explain to your pupils the steps they need to follow to recognize fallacies:

1. Read the statement carefully.
2. Decide if the statement is true.
3. If it is not true, figure out why.

STEP THREE Demonstrate the Skill

Ask pupils to watch and listen as you identify a fallacy, following Step Two. **SUGGESTION:** Write an *either/or* statement on the board—*Either you love volleyball, or you hate it.* Read the statement aloud and tell pupils it is incorrect. Identify what makes it false—*that some pupils like volleyball, but it is not their favorite sport. Others may not particularly like volleyball, but they don't hate it.* Point out that the statement could be made true by making the following change—*Some pupils love volleyball, while others hate it.*

STEP FOUR Practice the Skill

Use pages 73–76. See *Teacher Note* on each page.

STEP FIVE Provide Feedback

Discuss pupils' answers. **METACOGNITION:** Ask pupils to describe what they did. You may need to ask: **How did you change a fallacy to make it true? How did you choose the best slanted argument? How did you choose the correct analogy?**

ENRICHMENT ACTIVITIES

Challenge pupils to rewrite the following paragraph, underlining possible fallacies: *Everyone likes to go to the beach. But don't go on Sunday. It always rains on Sunday. Poplar Beach is the best beach. Nobody likes to go anyplace else.*

Have pupils correct the following fallacies. The corrections are in parentheses. *Milk* is to *cow* as *nest (egg)* is to *hen; thread* is to *needle* as *write (ink)* is to *pen; train* is to *track* as *car* is to *drive (road).*

Discuss examples of rationalizations, such as *Mrs. Smith thinks I should do better work, but no one can satisfy her; I lost my bike, but people lose bikes all the time.* Have pupils write three other examples of rationalizations.

UNIT 5

Synthesizing

BLOOM'S TAXONOMY

KNOWLEDGE	COMPREHENSION	APPLICATION	ANALYSIS	SYNTHESIS	EVALUATION

SYNTHESIS is the term used in Bloom's Taxonomy for the fifth stage in cognitive development. Synthesis is the ability to combine existing elements in order to create something original.

The authors of this program have identified the following skills as being particularly helpful in developing Bloom's fifth stage:

1. Communicating Ideas
2. Planning Projects
3. Building Hypotheses
4. Drawing Conclusions
5. Proposing Alternatives

Step-by-step procedures for teaching each of these skills follow. These lesson plans will help you use the program with ease as you incorporate ***thinking skills*** into your teaching day. Enrichment activities that accompany each lesson will help your students apply their newly acquired thinking skills to a variety of situations.

After this unit has been completed, copy and distribute the School-Home Newsletter on page T-46.

SKILL 25 PAGES 80–82 Communicating Ideas

STEP ONE Define the Skill

Discuss with your pupils the meaning of *communicating ideas:* **putting information or ideas into a form that will help others understand it.**

STEP TWO Identify the Steps

Explain to your pupils the steps they need to follow to communicate ideas:

1. Determine what your message is.
2. Choose the most appropriate way to share it.
3. Put the information or ideas in a form that will be understood by others.

STEP THREE Demonstrate the Skill

Ask pupils to watch and listen as you model a way to communicate ideas, following Step Two. **SUGGESTION:** Read this poem—*The Lizard is a timid thing/That cannot dance or fly or sing;/He hunts for bugs beneath the floor/And longs to be a dinosaur.* Tell pupils that a writer named John Gardner wanted to communicate his idea of what it is like to be a lizard. The form of communication he chose was poetry. If a writer wanted instead to explain carefully how a lizard looked, where it lived, and what it ate, the writer would probably choose the form of an encyclopedia article or science report to communicate that information.

STEP FOUR Practice the Skill

Use pages 80–82. See *Teacher Note* on each page.

STEP FIVE Provide Feedback

Discuss pupils' answers. **METACOGNITION:** Ask pupils to describe what they did. You may need to ask: **What did you do to understand the ideas in each form of communication? Did you change the way you read from one form to another?**

ENRICHMENT ACTIVITIES

Ask pupils to write their opinions on a controversial issue, such as *Should pupils plan cafeteria menus?* Provide a *yes* box and a *no* box in which pupils place a written reason for their choice. Allow volunteers to read what they have written.

Give pupils an informational pamphlet. Then ask pupils to design a chart that lists the key ideas in the pamphlet.

Have pupils discuss symbols that communicate ideas. For example: *A dove means peace; A heart means love; A skull-and-crossbones means poison.* Then challenge pupils to draw their own symbol and explain its meaning.

SKILL 26 PAGES 83–86 Planning Projects

STEP ONE Define the Skill

Discuss with your pupils the meaning of ***planning projects:*** **organizing materials, time, and effort to accomplish a goal.**

STEP TWO Identify the Steps

Explain to your pupils the steps they need to follow to plan a project:

1. Identify the goal—what you want to accomplish.
2. Figure out the steps you must take.
3. List the materials you will need.
4. Decide how much time you will need.

STEP THREE Demonstrate the Skill

Ask pupils to watch and listen as you plan a project, following Step Two. **SUGGESTION:** Present this situation to pupils—*You are assigned a science project for which you must show that plants need water and light.* That is the goal. List on the board the steps that must be taken—*prepare a plant that gets enough water and light, one that gets enough light but not water, and one that gets enough water but not light; then observe what happens.* Next list the materials you will need—*three plants of the same kind and same size in pots, a source of water, and a source of light.* Then estimate the amount of time each step will take.

STEP FOUR Practice the Skill

Use pages 83–86. See *Teacher Note* on each page.

STEP FIVE Provide Feedback

Discuss pupils' answers. **METACOGNITION:** Ask pupils to describe what they did. You may need to ask: **How did you decide which steps must be taken? the materials you need? the time that must be spent?**

ENRICHMENT ACTIVITIES

Have the class brainstorm suggestions for a real or imaginary field trip. After a choice has been made, let pupils outline the plans that must be made and decide who will do the necessary tasks.

Plan a class mural tied to a social studies unit. Let pupils work together in groups to complete sections of the mural. Direct groups to plan how to handle their section.

Have the class pretend it has a $200 budget to plant flowers around the school. Ask pupils to research and plan how they would spend the money.

SKILL 27 PAGES 87–90 Building Hypotheses

STEP ONE Define the Skill

Discuss with your pupils the meaning of ***building hypotheses:*** **forming possible explanations for events.**

STEP TWO Identify the Steps

Explain to your pupils the steps they need to follow to build a hypothesis:

1. Decide what needs to be explained.
2. Study the information you have.
3. Find connections between what needs to be explained and what you know has happened in the past.
4. Suggest a possible explanation.

STEP THREE Demonstrate the Skill

Ask pupils to watch and listen as you build a hypothesis, following Step Two. SUGGESTION: Present this situation to pupils—*You are riding along on your bike when you suddenly come across some shattered glass on the pavement. You don't have time to swerve and miss it. A day later, you're riding your bike again when the front tire deflates. Based on what you know has happened in the past, you can suggest a hypothesis, or possible explanation, for the flat tire—a piece of glass that you rode over earlier pierced the tire, and a leak resulted. You can check your hypothesis by carefully examining the tire.*

STEP FOUR Practice the Skill

Use pages 87–90. See *Teacher Note* on each page.

STEP FIVE Provide Feedback

Discuss pupils' answers. **METACOGNITION:** Ask pupils to describe what they did. You may need to ask: **Can additional facts cause you to change your hypothesis? What were the facts that supported each hypothesis?**

ENRICHMENT ACTIVITIES

Have a volunteer state a hypothesis and challenge the class to change it as you add new information. For example: *A man is riding a horse.* (He is a police officer/jockey.) *He is very tall.* (He is a police officer.)

Pupils might enjoy reading books, such as *Strange Mysteries from Around the World* by Seymour Simon. Have pupils discuss these unusual occurrences and offer their own hypotheses.

Have pupils work in groups to draw a treasure map. Direct them to locate the treasure within a specific distance from the school. Then have groups exchange maps and use the clues to determine the location of the treasures.

SKILL 28 PAGES 91–96 Drawing Conclusions

STEP ONE Define the Skill

Discuss with your pupils the meaning of ***drawing conclusions:*** **using facts about a situation to infer a general truth.**

STEP TWO Identify the Steps

Explain to your pupils the steps they need to follow to draw a conclusion:

1. Study the situation carefully. Look at all the information you have about it.

2. Think of a general statement—a conclusion—that must also be true about the situation.

STEP THREE Demonstrate the Skill

Ask pupils to watch and listen as you draw a conclusion, following Step Two. **SUGGESTION:** Write the following paragraph on the board—*Every year thousands of children are hurt on skateboards. They suffer from skinned knees and elbows to serious head injuries. In most injury cases, no protective gear was worn. When a skateboarder wears pads and a helmet, the risk of injury dramatically decreases.* Note that all the facts in the paragraph explain the relationship between skateboarding and injuries. From those pieces of information, you can draw the conclusion that using a skateboard without protective gear is dangerous.

STEP FOUR Practice the Skill

Use pages 91–96. See *Teacher Note* on each page.

STEP FIVE Provide Feedback

Discuss pupils' answers. **METACOGNITION:** Ask pupils to describe what they did. You may need to ask: **How did you draw the conclusions that you did? What facts did you consider when you were drawing your conclusions?**

ENRICHMENT ACTIVITIES

Present pupils with a statement and see how many conclusions they can draw. For example, *no horses at the farm are brown.* Possibilities include: *There may be several black horses. All the horses could be tan. Every horse could be a different color.*

Read brief selections from books that describe famous discoveries and the people who made them. Challenge pupils to draw conclusions about these people.

Pupils may enjoy discussing favorite TV programs and drawing conclusions about the plot or characters.

SKILL 29 PAGES 97–102 Proposing Alternatives

STEP ONE Define the Skill

Discuss with your pupils the meaning of ***proposing alternatives:*** **suggesting possible solutions to a problem.**

STEP TWO Identify the Steps

Explain to your pupils the steps they need to follow to propose alternatives:

1. Identify the problem.
2. Brainstorm as many solutions as you can.
3. Decide which solutions are possible and practical.

STEP THREE Demonstrate the Skill

Ask pupils to watch and listen as you propose alternatives for solving a problem, following Step Two. **SUGGESTION:** Present a problem to the class—*The boy who sits next to Maria taps his pencil as he does his work. The noise disturbs Maria.* Consider possible solutions—*Maria can try to ignore the noise, she can tell the teacher, she can tell the boy that he is rude, or she can politely ask the boy to stop.*

STEP FOUR Practice the Skill

Use pages 97–102. See *Teacher Note* on each page.

STEP FIVE Provide Feedback

Discuss pupils' answers. **METACOGNITION:** Ask pupils to describe what they did. You may need to ask: **What helped you think of different solutions? How would you choose the best solution in each case?**

ENRICHMENT ACTIVITIES

Use a lesson from a social studies unit to determine possible alternatives to an historic act. For example: *What other action might the colonists have taken in place of the Boston Tea Party?*

Direct pupils to develop a report on a book they have read. Have them propose alternative formats for the report.

Encourage volunteers to discuss a real or fanciful problem they are experiencing. Challenge the class to propose alternative solutions to the problem.

UNIT 6

Evaluating

BLOOM'S TAXONOMY

KNOWLEDGE	COMPREHENSION	APPLICATION	ANALYSIS	SYNTHESIS	EVALUATION

EVALUATION is the term used in Bloom's Taxonomy for the sixth stage in cognitive development. This final stage involves the ability to make a judgment about the value of something by using a standard.

The authors of this program have identified the following skills as being particularly helpful in developing Bloom's final stage:

1. Testing Generalizations
2. Developing Criteria
3. Judging Accuracy
4. Making Decisions
5. Identifying Values
6. Interpreting the Mood of a Story

Step-by-step procedures for teaching each of these skills follow. These lesson plans will help you use the program with ease as you incorporate ***thinking skills*** into your teaching day. Enrichment activities that accompany each lesson will help your students apply their newly acquired thinking skills to a variety of situations.

After this unit has been completed, copy and distribute the School-Home Newsletter on page T-47.

SKILL 30 PAGES 106–108 Testing Generalizations

STEP ONE Define the Skill

Discuss with your pupils the meaning of ***testing generalizations:*** **determining whether a general statement is true all the time.**

STEP TWO Identify the Steps

Explain to your pupils the steps they need to follow to test a generalization:

1. Read the generalization carefully.
2. Look for evidence or occasions that prove the generalization false.

STEP THREE Demonstrate the Skill

Ask pupils to watch and listen as you test a generalization, following Step Two. **SUGGESTION:** Write the following spelling generalization on the board—*Change the* f *or* fe *to* v *and add* -es *to form the plural of words ending with a single* f *or with* fe. Write words on the board that follow this rule—*loaf, loaves; life, lives; thief, thieves*. Explain that the generalization might always be true, but you don't have enough evidence to be sure. Write additional words ending in *f* or *fe* on the board, including the word *chief* and its plural, *chiefs*. Note that *chief* proves the generalization is not always true.

STEP FOUR Practice the Skill

Use pages 106–108. See *Teacher Note* on each page.

STEP FIVE Provide Feedback

Discuss pupils' answers. **METACOGNITION:** Ask pupils to describe what they did. You may need to ask: **How did you choose the correct generalization? What ways did you use to disprove generalizations?**

ENRICHMENT ACTIVITIES

Ask pupils to make and test generalizations about the following: *The scores for Saturday's baseball games are: Newton – 6, Smithville – 1; Jackson Heights – 2, Grant – 0.*

Pupils may enjoy keeping a log of generalizations they hear on TV programs or commercials. The generalizations may then be tested by the class.

Present pupils with several generalizations that are not true, such as *Young people today are rude; Watching television is a waste of time; Kids like to ride rollercoasters.* Have pupils rewrite each generalization to make it true.

SKILL 31 PAGES 109–112 Developing Criteria

STEP ONE Define the Skill

Discuss with your pupils the meaning of ***developing criteria:*** **deciding on rules or guidelines to use in making judgments.**

STEP TWO Identify the Steps

Explain to your pupils the steps they need to follow to develop criteria:

1. Ask yourself what you need to do.
2. Think of criteria—rules or guidelines—that will help you judge which of your choices will best meet your needs.
3. Use the criteria to make your judgment.

STEP THREE Demonstrate the Skill

Ask pupils to watch and listen as you develop criteria, following Step Two. **SUGGESTION:** Present this situation to the class—*You're going on a camping trip, and you need to decide what clothes to pack.* List on the board the criteria that could be used to make that decision—*The clothes should be comfortable and not easily wrinkled; you should bring enough lightweight clothes to add layer upon layer on chilly nights; keep in mind that you might go swimming and also that it may rain; you should not pack too many clothes—just enough for each day you'll be gone*. Next, list items of clothing on the board, such as *jeans, skirt or dress pants, loafers, sneakers, swimming suit, sweatshirt, rain poncho, winter coat, frilly clothes or dress shirt, T-shirts, scarf*. Use the criteria to judge which clothes should be packed.

STEP FOUR Practice the Skill

Use pages 109–112. See *Teacher Note* on each page.

STEP FIVE Provide Feedback

Discuss pupils' answers. **METACOGNITION:** Ask pupils to describe what they did. You may need to ask: **How did you use the rules, or criteria, to make your judgment? What helped you choose your own criteria?**

ENRICHMENT ACTIVITIES

Have pupils write and compare criteria that might be used to select a basketball player to the criteria that might be used to select a football player.

Tell pupils they will be sailing across the ocean. Have them develop criteria for judging the supplies that should be taken.

Explain that Nellie Bly was a newspaper reporter who faked insanity so she could describe conditions in mental hospitals. Ask students to describe the qualities a person would need to be successful at this kind of work.

SKILL 32 PAGES 113–116 Judging Accuracy

STEP ONE Define the Skill

Discuss with your pupils the meaning of ***judging accuracy:*** **evaluating whether a statement is correct and exact.**

STEP TWO Identify the Steps

Explain to your pupils the steps they need to follow to judge the accuracy of a statement:

1. Figure out the main idea of what you are reading.
2. Check to see that each sentence is logical and could be true.
3. Make sure that one idea does not contradict another.
4. Determine whether the words explain or describe things exactly.
5. Ask yourself where you can check to make sure the information is right. If necessary, check a reference book.

STEP THREE Demonstrate the Skill

Ask pupils to watch and listen as you judge the accuracy of a statement, following Step Two.

SUGGESTION: Write the following paragraph on the board—*In Mexico, the sun shines all the time. It's nice and hot and dry there, so everybody is happy. Even when it rains, people are still happy.* Point out that the first statement is not exact. Much of Mexico may have a hot, dry climate, but nowhere does the sun shine "all the time." The second sentence draws an illogical conclusion. The third sentence contradicts the first. Make the appropriate judgment—the paragraph is not accurately written.

STEP FOUR Practice the Skill

Use pages 113–116. See *Teacher Note* on each page.

STEP FIVE Provide Feedback

Discuss pupils' answers. **METACOGNITION:** Ask pupils to describe what they did. You may need to ask: **What helped you decide one statement contradicted another? How did you decide a conclusion was not logical? How did you decide which details were exact, specific, and accurate?**

ENRICHMENT ACTIVITIES

Tape a broadcast of fans' reactions to their sports team. Ask pupils to note all words and phrases that may not be completely accurate. For example, in the sentence *The coach always picked Martin*, the use of *always* may be inaccurate. Challenge pupils to write a factual account of the event eliminating any inaccuracies.

Have pupils identify the inaccuracies in the following paragraph: *When the light turned red, traffic started to move. It was 6:15, so I had 20 minutes to get there by 6:30. It was hard to see. The wipers weren't working, and the sun was in my eyes.*

Ask pupils to rate and discuss the accuracy of the following sources of weather predictions: *The Farmer's Almanac*, old wives' tales, meteorologist/weather satellite.

SKILL 33 PAGES 117–120 Making Decisions

STEP ONE Define the Skill

Discuss with your pupils the meaning of ***making decisions:*** **choosing a course of action after carefully considering the alternatives.**

STEP TWO Identify the Steps

Explain to your pupils the steps they need to follow to make a decision:

1. Study the situation.
2. Brainstorm possible courses of action.
3. Use rules (criteria) to choose the best action.
4. Be prepared to explain why you decided as you did.

STEP THREE Demonstrate the Skill

Ask pupils to watch and listen as you make a decision, following Step Two. **SUGGESTION:** Present the following situation to the class—*You telephone a sick friend, who says he has to stay in bed all day and is bored.* List possible courses of action—*deciding he's not a good friend; taking him a jigsaw puzzle; lending him your rollerblades; taking him a book to read.* Choose the action that best fits the situation—*the book.* Explain why the other actions do not make as much sense.

STEP FOUR Practice the Skill

Use pages 117–120. See *Teacher Note* on each page.

STEP FIVE Provide Feedback

Discuss pupils' answers. **METACOGNITION:** Ask pupils to describe what they did. You may need to ask: **How did you decide on evidence or sources to back up decisions?**

ENRICHMENT ACTIVITIES

Have pupils list emergency situations and then ask them to decide which things are most important and must be handled immediately.

Ask pupils to decide where they would want to live if they could choose anywhere in the world. Ask them to explain the reasons for their choice.

Let groups of pupils decide what they would like to do for a language arts project. For example, they may decide to put on a play, write a story, make a book of favorite poems and draw illustrations for them.

SKILL 34 PAGES 121–124 Identifying Values

STEP ONE Define the Skill

Discuss with your pupils the meaning of ***identifying values:*** **recognizing a person's beliefs or feelings about what is right.**

STEP TWO Identify the Steps

Explain to your pupils the steps they need to follow to identify values:

1. Study the situation.
2. Ask yourself: What is the right thing to do in this situation?
3. If you are reading about another person, ask yourself: What does this person think is the right thing to do? Is that the same thing I think?

STEP THREE Demonstrate the Skill

Ask pupils to watch and listen as you identify values, following Step Two. **SUGGESTION:** Write this paragraph on the board—*Matthew and Lynn were choosing teams for a neighborhood soccer game. Soon only a few children remained unselected. Lynn noticed one of them—a small kid named Marcus who was always picked last. Marcus looked uncomfortable. Lynn started to call out Marti Moore's name, then called Marcus's instead.* Show pupils how you can infer from Lynn's actions that she believes we should be considerate of other people's feelings and help others feel good about themselves. Consideration is a value that guided Lynn's behavior.

STEP FOUR Practice the Skill

Use pages 121–124. See *Teacher Note* on each page.

STEP FIVE Provide Feedback

Discuss pupils' answers. **METACOGNITION:** Ask pupils to describe what they did. You may need to ask: **What clues helped you identify the value conflict? Why did you choose the solution you did?**

ENRICHMENT ACTIVITIES

Suggest that small groups of pupils read biographies and discuss the values held by the person discussed in each book.

Challenge pupils to design posters that describe the importance of conservation or ecology. Encourage them to depict values, such as an appreciation of beauty, clean air and water, or an understanding of the ecosystems.

Discuss criteria for giving sports awards. For example: *Should improvement over the season be rewarded? fair play? individual effort? daily attendance at practice?*

SKILL 35 PAGES 125–126 Mood of a Story

STEP ONE Define the Skill

Discuss with your pupils the meaning of identifying the ***mood of a story:* identifying the main feeling or emotion created by a story.**

STEP TWO Identify the Steps

Explain to your pupils the steps they need to follow to identify the mood of a story:

1. Look for words that set the tone or express a feeling.
2. Relate all these words to identify the overall feeling the whole story creates.

STEP THREE Demonstrate the Skill

Ask pupils to watch and listen as you find the mood of a story, following Step Two. **SUGGESTION:** Write this paragraph on the board—*The jury filed back into the courtroom, one by one. Several looked directly at Tom Brach, the defendant, while others avoided eye contact. The courtroom quieted. You could hear the clock ticking. Then the voice of the judge boomed, "Ladies and gentlemen of the jury, have you reached a verdict?"* Note the words *one by one, quieted, ticking,* and *boomed.* Also note the situation—*a trial about to end, the verdict about to be read, some jurors avoiding the defendant.* Explain how these words and details help create a mood of tension and suspense in the story.

STEP FOUR Practice the Skill

Use pages 125–126. See *Teacher Note* on each page.

STEP FIVE Provide Feedback

Discuss pupils' answers. **METACOGNITION:** Ask pupils to describe what they did. You may need to ask: **Which clues helped you identify the mood?**

ENRICHMENT ACTIVITIES

Challenge pupils to write questions to a favorite story character. For example: *How did the character feel when certain events took place?* Have pupils exchange papers and write a response to their partner's questions.

Challenge pupils to describe a character using adjectives and adverbs to establish a mood. For example, instead of simply saying a person is poor, pupils should write, *The frightened girl was desperately hungry, shivering in the frigid air.*

Discuss the mood of a particular story. Then consider how the story might have been different had one of the characters been a different kind of person. Would the same problem have existed? Would other characters have reacted the same way?

Class Assessment Summary

TEACHER

SCHOOL GRADE

Directions: Daily observation and planned activities help determine whether students have achieved mastery of a particular skill. Indicate each student's mastery of a skill by writing the date in the corresponding box.

	UNIT 1: KNOWING					UNIT 2: UNDERSTANDING						
	Classifying	Real and Fanciful	Fact and Opinion	Definition and Example	Outlining and Summarizing	Comparing and Contrasting	Identifying Structure	Steps in a Process	Figural Relationships	Comparing Word Meanings	Identifying Main Ideas	Identifying Relationships
NAMES SKILLS ▶	1	2	3	4	5	6	7	8	9	10	11	12

Class Assessment Summary

TEACHER

SCHOOL GRADE

Directions: Daily observation and planned activities help determine whether students have achieved mastery of a particular skill. Indicate each student's mastery of a skill by writing the date in the corresponding box.

	UNIT 3: APPLYING					UNIT 4: ANALYZING						
	Ordering Objects	Estimating	Anticipating Probabilities	Inferring	Changes in Word Meanings	Judging Completeness	Relevance of Information	Abstract or Concrete	Logic of Actions	Elements of a Selection	Story Logic	Recognizing Fallacies
NAMES / SKILLS ▸	13	14	15	16	17	18	19	20	21	22	23	24

Class Assessment Summary

TEACHER

SCHOOL GRADE

Directions: Daily observation and planned activities help determine whether students have achieved mastery of a particular skill. Indicate each student's mastery of a skill by writing the date in the corresponding box.

	UNIT 5: SYNTHESIZING					UNIT 6: EVALUATING					
	Communicating Ideas	Planning Projects	Building Hypotheses	Drawing Conclusions	Proposing Alternatives	Testing Generalizations	Developing Criteria	Judging Accuracy	Making Decisions	Identifying Values	Mood of a Story
NAMES SKILLS ▸	25	26	27	28	29	30	31	32	33	34	35

Thinker's Corner

SCHOOL–HOME NEWSLETTER

UNIT 1

KNOWING

In the first unit of *Critical Thinking: Reading, Thinking, and Reasoning Skills,* your child has been studying the following skills:

- classifying
- real and fanciful
- fact and opinion
- definition and example
- outlining and summarizing

This newsletter is designed to provide an important link between home and school. You can support your child's learning habits by asking what he or she has learned in school and by discussing papers brought home. You may also wish to do some of the activities suggested in this newsletter.

What Style Is Your Style?

To help your child practice classifying, encourage him or her to find examples of different styles of music. Together, decide which styles to investigate, such as rock and roll, blues, classical, and folk music. Then have your child list song titles that fit each category. Check the different sections of a music store to get suggestions for titles.

Radio XYZ

Now that you've identified different styles of music, have fun with your child making up call letters for a radio station to broadcast those songs. Examples might include WRNR (for rock and roll), KTRY (for country), or KLSS (for classical). Have your child make a list of five songs he or she would play as disk jockey on the station.

Radio Fancy

While you've got on your make-believe radio station, ask your child to make up an old time radio drama. Suggest a fanciful character like Space Boy or Spider Woman. Since the characters are fanciful, make up something special only he or she can do.

How Do You Describe It?

Ask your child to make a list of three or four interesting words he or she has read lately. Think of how those words might be used to describe or explain something. Challenge your child to use the words in a paragraph.

Ready to Report

Ask your child to pretend he or she is going to write a report about plants. Ask how an outline might help your child prepare the report. For example, suggest that your child complete the following outline. Possible answers are in parentheses.

I. Plants
   A. (Characteristics)
   B. (Seedless Plants)
   C. (Seed Plants)
II. Plant Processes
   A. (Photosynthesis)
   B. (Respiration)

Thinker's Corner

SCHOOL–HOME NEWSLETTER

UNIT 2

UNDERSTANDING

In the second unit of ***Critical Thinking: Reading, Thinking, and Reasoning Skills,*** your child has been studying the following skills:

- comparing and contrasting
- identifying structure
- steps in a process
- figural relationships
- comparing word meanings
- identifying main ideas
- identifying relationships

This newsletter is designed to provide an important link between home and school. You can support your child's learning habits by asking what he or she has learned in school and by discussing papers brought home. You may also wish to do some of the activities suggested in this newsletter.

Alike and Different

Ask your child to tell how the following items are alike and different:

- typewriter and computer
- telephone and postcard
- movie and video

Be an Architect

Work with your child to design a house, a store, or a recreation center. First draw a floor plan. Identify the various rooms, what they are used for, and what's in them. Then draw a picture of the front of the building that you're designing.

How Do You Do It?

Imagine that you and your child have a chance to build the building you just designed in the "Be an Architect" activity. Discuss the steps it would take to complete the building. For example, first you have to find a place to build. Then you need to clear the land, lay out the plan, and pour a foundation. Find out more about building by checking out a book from the library to share with your child.

Chart Your Time

Help your child understand figural relationships by making a bar graph. Ask your child to use the chart below to make a bar graph that shows how many hours he or she watches TV, spends on homework, or plays with friends. If necessary, review bar graphs with your child by showing examples from a math text, newspaper, or other source.

5							
4							
3							
2							
1							
	Mon	Tue	Wed	Thu	Fri	Sat	Sun

From Al to Zeal

What do the words *call*, *eventual*, and *dally* have in common? They all contain the letters *al*. Have fun with your child trying to think of a word with *al* starting with each letter of the alphabet.

Thinker's Corner

SCHOOL–HOME NEWSLETTER

UNIT 3

APPLYING

In the third unit of ***Critical Thinking: Reading, Thinking, and Reasoning Skills,*** your child has been studying the following skills:

- ordering objects
- estimating
- anticipating probabilities
- inferring
- changes in word meanings

This newsletter is designed to provide an important link between home and school. You can support your child's learning habits by asking what he or she has learned in school and by discussing papers brought home. You may also wish to do some of the activities suggested in this newsletter.

How Far?

Have your child make a list of the names of five or six large cities. Then ask him or her to list them in order of closest to farthest from where you live. Provide a map for your child to use if he or she is uncertain of each city's location.

How Long Will It Take?

Have your child choose one of the cities mentioned in the above activity and estimate how long it would take to drive there. Suggest that your child use the scale on a map to check his or her estimate.

The Year 2001

With your child, make some predictions about what life will be like in the year 2001. Discuss what things might be different. Have your child write and illustrate what one day in his or her life might be like. Encourage your child to share his or her writing with other family members.

Before and After

To *infer* means to make decisions about things that may have happened. Find an interesting picture in a magazine or newspaper, such as one that advertises an upcoming movie. Ask your child to tell what he or she thinks happened before the scene that is pictured. Then ask what might happen right after the scene. Provide your child with drawing materials and ask your child to draw both scenes. Encourage your child to label each picture and to write a short paragraph that tells the story that goes with the pictures.

Word Word

Look at the list of words below. Each word has at least two meanings. Ask your child to tell two meanings. Then have him or her make up a sentence that uses both meanings of the word. Have your child write and illustrate each sentence.

trunk	trunk
park	park
type	type

Thinker's Corner

SCHOOL–HOME NEWSLETTER

UNIT 4

ANALYZING

In the fourth unit of ***Critical Thinking: Reading, Thinking, and Reasoning Skills,*** your child has been studying the following skills:

- judging completeness
- relevance of information
- abstract or concrete
- logic of actions
- elements of a selection
- story logic
- recognizing fallacies

This newsletter is designed to provide an important link between home and school. You can support your child's learning habits by asking what he or she has learned in school and by discussing papers brought home. You may also wish to do some of the activities suggested in this newsletter.

What's Important?

Help your child discuss relevance of information by having him or her pretend to prepare for a vacation. The vacation is to a state that you have never visited before. Discuss what kinds of things would be important to know, such as what the weather is like. Also discuss what might be less important to know, such as how many people live in the state.

A Ladder of My Pet

Help your child work with abstract and concrete words. Ask him or her to make a ladder about a real or an imaginary pet, similar to the example. Begin with the pet's name at the bottom. Gradually fill in more general terms to get to the broadest term of "living thing."

living thing
animal
mammal
pet
feline
cat
Slate

Story Elements

You can help your child understand the elements of a selection as shown below. Encourage your child to think about a book he or she has recently read and then copy and complete the chart.

Elements of a Selection	
characters	
setting	
problem or goal	
climax	
solution	

Story Logic

Some stories begin in the present and then flash back to an earlier time to tell a story. If your child has difficulty with the concept of flashback, read *The Midnight Fox* by Betsy Byars or *Where the Red Fern Grows* by Wilson Rawls. Discuss how each author used the flashback technique. Then help your child tell a story with a "flashback."

Thinker's Corner

SCHOOL–HOME NEWSLETTER

UNIT 5

SYNTHESIZING

In the fifth unit of ***Critical Thinking: Reading, Thinking, and Reasoning Skills,*** your child has been studying the following skills:

- communicating ideas
- planning projects
- building hypotheses
- drawing conclusions
- proposing alternatives

This newsletter is designed to provide an important link between home and school. You can support your child's learning habits by asking what he or she has learned in school and by discussing papers brought home. You may also wish to do some of the activities suggested in this newsletter.

A Picture Story

One way of communicating ideas is through a rebus story. A rebus is a picture that stands for a word. Challenge your child to draw a rebus sentence for family members to identify. Example:

I need your book.

You're the Director

Have fun helping your child plan a project. Have your child pretend that he or she is making a music video. Ask him or her to make a list of things that will be needed, such as music, scenery, actions to tell the story of the song, and a camera.

Why Do You Think This Is True?

The skill of building hypotheses helps your child learn to form possible explanations for things that happen. Ask your child to give at least two reasons to support the hypothesis *Many people prefer train travel to airplane travel.*

Drawing Conclusions

As children learn to make decisions about situations, they need to take the time to examine all the information they have regarding that situation. You can help your child practice drawing conclusions by asking him or her to tell what happened in the following situation: *A man and a dog are walking down the street. The dog stops and refuses to cross the street. The man urges the dog on, but the dog doesn't move. Soon a car zooms by. Then the dog moves on. Why did the dog know to stop but the man did not?* (The man was blind; the dog was a guide dog.)

What Are Your Alternatives?

Discuss with your child what to do in some situations that may cause problems for him or her. For example, ask what alternatives are available if someone is suspiciously following him or her, if someone offers drugs, or if someone wants help in cheating.

Thinker's Corner

SCHOOL–HOME NEWSLETTER

UNIT 6

EVALUATING

In the sixth unit of ***Critical Thinking: Reading, Thinking, and Reasoning Skills,*** your child has been studying the following skills:

- testing generalizations
- developing criteria
- judging accuracy
- making decisions
- identifying values
- mood of a story

This newsletter is designed to provide an important link between home and school. You can support your child's learning habits by asking what he or she has learned in school and by discussing papers brought home. You may also wish to do some of the activities suggested in this newsletter.

Writing Haiku

Haiku poetry follows this criteria:

- A haiku has three lines.
- The first and third lines each have five syllables.
- The second line has seven syllables.
- Haiku does not rhyme.

Following the criteria, work with your child to write a haiku.

Is This True?

Help your child test generalizations by asking him or her to tell whether the following is true: *Handicapped people are unable to participate in sports.* Have your child explain why the statement is not true and how it can be proven false. Then ask your child to give a generalization for you to explain whether it's true.

You Decide

As children learn to make decisions, they need to take the time to study information and consider alternatives. You can help your child practice making decisions by asking what he or she would do in the following situation: *You have been asked to baby-sit your neighbor's little boy. You wanted to spend the night at your friend's house. However, you need money to buy a computer game you want. What will you decide?*

Identifying Values

Suppose your child has agreed to take the baby-sitting job described in the previous activity but now doesn't want to do it. Discuss with your child what is the right thing to do. Should your child: *take the job anyway, call and explain why you don't want to do it, or call and say an emergency has come up (even though it hasn't)?*

What's the Mood?

Readers may experience happiness, fear, laughter, or sadness by reading a good story. You can help your child understand the mood of a story by asking questions such as those below. Ask your child to tell about a favorite story he or she has read recently.

1. *How did the story make you feel?*
2. *What words in the story made you feel that way?*
3. *How do you think the characters felt?*

NOTES

STECK-VAUGHN

CRITICAL THINKING

Reading, Thinking, and Reasoning Skills

Authors

Don Barnes
Professor of Education
Ball State University; Muncie, Indiana

Arlene Burgdorf
Former Resource Consultant
Hammond Indiana Public Schools

L. Stanley Wenck
Professor of Educational Psychology
Ball State University; Muncie, Indiana

Consultant

Gloria Sesso
Supervisor of Social Studies
Half Hollow Hills School District; Dix Hills, New York

LEVEL

A	B	C	D	E	F

www.steck-vaughn.com

ACKNOWLEDGMENTS

Executive Editor: Elizabeth Strauss

Project Editor: Anita Arndt

Consulting Editor: Melinda Veatch

Design, Production, and Editorial Services: The Quarasan Group, Inc.

Contributing Writers: Tara McCarthy, Linda Ward Beech

Cover Design: Linda Adkins Graphic Design

Text:
Every effort has been made to trace the ownership of all copyrighted material and to secure the necessary permission to reprint these selections. In the event of any question arising as to the use of any material, the editor and publisher, while expressing regret for any inadvertent error, will be happy to make the necessary correction in future printings.

"An old silent pond" from CRICKET SONGS, Japanese haiku translated by Harry Behn. Copyright © 1964 by Harry Behn. Copyright © 1992 renewed. Reprinted by permission of Marian Reiner.

"The Bird of the Night" reprinted with permission of Macmillan Publishing Company from THE BAT-POET by Randall Jarrell. Copyright © Macmillan Publishing Company 1963, 1964. Copyrights © renewed 1991, 1992.

Specified excerpt on page 13 of Chapter III in CHARLOTTE'S WEB by E. B. White. Copyright © 1952, by E. B. White. Renewed © 1980 by E. B. White. Reprinted by permission of HarperCollins Publishers and Hamish Hamilton, Ltd.

Paragraphs reprinted from THE CORAL REEF by Gilda Berger, text copyright © 1977 by Gilda Berger. Reprinted with permission from the author.

Riddle and excerpt from THE HOBBIT by J. R. R. Tolkien. Copyright © 1966 by J. R. R. Tolkien. Reprinted by permission of Houghton Mifflin Company and HarperCollins UK. All rights reserved.

"Message from a Caterpillar" from LITTLE RACCOON AND POEMS FROM THE WOODS by Lilian Moore. Text copyright © 1975 by Lillian Moore. All rights reserved. Reprinted by permission of Marian Reiner for the author.

Excerpt from A NATURAL HISTORY OF NEW YORK CITY by John Kiernan. Copyright © 1959 by John Francis Kiernan. Reprinted by permission of Houghton Mifflin Company. All rights reserved.

Pictures to Read from PICK A PECK OF PUZZLES by Arnold Roth. Copyright © 1966 by Scholastic Book Services. Reprinted by permission of the author.

Excerpt from "The Runaway" from THE POETRY OF ROBERT FROST edited by Edward Connery Lathem. Copyright 1923, © 1969 by Holt, Rinehart and Winston. Copyright 1951 by Robert Frost. Reprinted by permission of Henry Holt and Company, Inc., the Estate of the author, and Jonathan Cape Publishers.

Codes adapted with permission of Macmillan Publishing Company from SECRET CODES AND CIPHERS by Joel Rothman and Ruthven Tremain. Copyright © 1969 by Joel Rothman and Ruthven Tremain.

Photography:
p. 5 — Rick Reinhard
p. 17 — Krantzen Studio Inc.
p. 18 top left — Stephen Dalton/Animals Animals
p. 18 top right — Runk /Schoenberger/Grant Heilman
p. 18 bottom left — Runk/Schoenberger/Grant Heilman
p. 18 bottom right — Grant Heilman Photography
p. 20 — George McCaul
p. 21 — Nita Winter
p. 39 — Bob Daemmrich/TexaStock
p. 41 — Kathy Sloane
p. 59 — H. Armstrong Roberts
p. 79 — Nita Winter
p. 82 — The Metropolitan Museum of Art
pp. 89, 96 — The Granger Collection
p. 101 — Harvy R. Phillips/PPI
p. 105 — Nita Winter
p. 127 — Photoworld/FPG
p. 128 — Phyllis Liedeker

Illustration:
pp. 12, 19, 22, 27, 43, 48, 49, 56, 68, 78, 118, 124 — Scott Bieser
pp. 26, 31, 36, 72, 92, 109 — Charles Varner/Carol Bancroft & Friends
pp. 28, 54, 55, 90, 99, 113, 114 — Keith Wilson
p. 40 — Linda Hawkins
pp. 87, 103, 104 — Lynn McClain

ISBN 0-8114-6604-3

TABLE OF CONTENTS

TABLE OF CONTENTS

UNIT 1

Knowing

Teacher Note

In order to develop Bloom's first stage—knowing—the pupil needs to engage in the following skills:

- Classifying
- Discriminating Between Real and Fanciful
- Discriminating Between Fact and Opinion
- Discriminating Between Definition and Example
- Outlining and Summarizing

Knowing means getting the facts together. Let's try it out. What's happening in this picture? What part of the bike is the man adjusting? Have you ever had to fix a tire on your bike? How did you know what to do?

Classifying

When you **classify,** you arrange things in groups according to their similarities. Read the following paragraphs and the chart that shows how foods are grouped.

What's your favorite food? Is it a plate of spicy spaghetti or a bowl of cool ice cream? Whatever your favorite food, it belongs to one of the food groups in the chart.

Next to each food group is the daily serving size suggested to maintain a healthful diet. You'll notice that foods containing fats, oils, and sweets should be eaten sparingly. So do your body a favor—snack on carrots instead of cookies!

FOOD GROUP	SERVINGS
A. Bread, Cereal, Rice, and Pasta	6-11
B. Vegetable	3-5
C. Fruit	2-4
D. Milk, Yogurt, and Cheese	2-3
E. Meat, Poultry, Fish, Dry Beans, Eggs, and Nuts	2-3
F. Fats, Oils, and Sweets	Use sparingly.

Source: Food Guide Pyramid, U.S. Department of Agriculture, May 1992.

Classify each food by writing the letter of the food group to which the food belongs.

1. apple ______C______
2. peanut ______E______
3. hamburger ______E______
4. noodles ______A______
5. cheese ______D______
6. broccoli ______B______
7. rice ______A______
8. butter ______F______
9. corn flakes ______A______
10. lettuce ______B______

If you eat a meal of spaghetti and meatballs with a green salad and a glass of milk, what food groups are included in your meal?

A, B, D, E

Name ____________________

Teacher Note
Ask pupils why they classified each food item as they did.

SKILL 1 Classifying

Usually, an item can be classified, or categorized, in more than one group. Each person listed below may be categorized as a member of someone's immediate family or as a relative. They also may be categorized as male or female and as members of the same generation or an older generation. Write the name of each person under all the headings of groups to which the person could belong. Some blank lines will not be used. Some answers may be used more than once.

aunt	cousin	brother	mother	grandmother	uncle
stepfather	stepmother	sister	grandfather	father	

Immediate Family

brother	sister
mother	father
stepfather	stepmother

Other Relatives

aunt	grandfather
cousin	uncle
grandmother	

Male

cousin	grandfather
brother	uncle
stepfather	father

Female

aunt	grandmother
cousin	sister
mother	stepmother

Same Generation as You

cousin	
brother	
sister	

Older Generation than You

aunt	grandfather
mother	uncle
stepfather	father
grandmother	stepmother

Name ______________________________

Teacher Note
Ask pupils to suggest other ways people could be classified.

Classifying

Writers often write about kinds, or classes, of things. When you read, you can note how items are classified. Read this article. Then classify each of the instruments mentioned in the article by writing its name under the correct heading below.

Listen to an orchestra, and you'll hear one beautiful, harmonious piece of music. That music is produced by a variety of musical instruments, from big **bass drums** to dainty **piccolos. Flutes** sing high melodies, while **tubas** blow low and deep. The delicate **triangle** tinkles, while **cellos** sound mournful. **Violins** produce a wide range of rich sounds.

Although there's a variety of instruments, there are actually only three main kinds of instruments—stringed, wind, and percussion. A stringed instrument produces sound when its strings are plucked or when a bow is moved across them. Just think of the sound you hear when someone strums a **guitar.** A wind instrument is played with the breath. Picture a **trumpet** player blowing into his or her horn. The percussion instruments are played by striking them. Just hear the clang of **cymbals.**

STRINGED	WIND	PERCUSSION
cellos	piccolos	bass drums
violins	flutes	triangle
guitar	tubas	cymbals
	trumpet	

To play the piano, you strike the keys. The keys, in turn, strike little hammers that cause strings to vibrate. In which two categories of musical instruments would you classify the piano? Why?

percussion and stringed: percussion because the piano keys are struck, and stringed because piano strings are moved by hammers

Name ______________________

Teacher Note
Have students explain why they classified each instrument as they did. Ask if they can add instruments to each classification.

Real and Fanciful

Many of the stories you read are **fiction,** or made up by the author. Yet they are usually about people who really could exist and events that really could happen. Some fiction, however, is **fantasy.** It concerns people and events that can only be imagined. Write two different stories—one **realistic** and one fantasy. If only one sentence is given, use it in both stories. For each pair of sentences, use one sentence in each story. Then, on a separate sheet of paper, complete each story with an appropriate ending.

Sentence 1: Daniel sat at the school's new computer and turned it on.

Sentence 2: The computer whirred, buzzed, clicked, and then showed a prompt sign.

Sentence 3:	Daniel inserted a disk and hit a few keys.	**OR**	Daniel thought he must be mistaken when he saw the keyboard typing by itself.
Sentence 4:	Then Daniel saw this message on the screen: "Wait till you see what I can do!"	**OR**	He had a great idea for a story.

Realistic Story Daniel sat at the school's new computer and turned it on. The computer whirred, buzzed, clicked, and then showed a prompt sign. Daniel inserted a disk and hit a few keys. He had a great idea for a story.

Fantasy Daniel sat at the school's new computer and turned it on. The computer whirred, buzzed, clicked, and then showed a prompt sign. Daniel thought he must be mistaken when he saw the keyboard typing by itself. Then Daniel saw this message on the screen: "Wait till you see what I can do!"

Name ________________

Teacher Note
Give pupils a chance to read their completed stories aloud to the class. Ask pupils to describe stories they have read that are realistic and stories that are fantasies.

SKILL 2 Real and Fanciful

People sometimes exaggerate to express strong feelings. For example, a person who says, "My mouth was on fire when I tasted that food," is reacting strongly to an unpleasant event. A simple statement of fact would be, "The taste of the strong, spicy food caused a burning sensation in my mouth."

Finish each sentence below by underlining the word or words in parentheses that will make the sentence a simple statement of fact.

1. There were (millions of, several, thousands of) mice scurrying around the old house.

2. When the branches of the old tree swayed, they (made a swishing sound, moaned and groaned, scared me to death).

3. The lights over the pond, which were probably caused by (UFO's, prowlers with flashlights, fireflies), gave me an eerie feeling as they twinkled off and on.

4. The winning wrestler won an amazing number of matches during his career. He won (five, 8 million, 105) matches.

5. The room is so cold that the temperature in here must be (zero, cold enough to freeze us to death, near freezing).

6. We saw a waterfall in the river that was (sky high, taller than an ant hill, as high as a redwood tree).

7. The new town hall will be (very beautiful, the finest in the land, the most impressive building in history).

8. The noise from the engine was loud enough to (split our eardrums, drive us crazy, almost deafen us for the moment).

9. My younger brother has grown (very rapidly, like a weed, by leaps and bounds).

10. She fell asleep in the noonday sun and woke up (with a sunburn, looking like a lobster, red as a beet).

Name ______________________________

Teacher Note
After pupils have completed the page, have them identify the choice in each sentence that would have made the statement the most fanciful. Stress again that strong feelings often lead us to exaggerate through fancy. Have pupils decide which strong feeling could lead a person to make a fanciful statement about the situation set forth in each sentence (*annoyance*, *fear*, *admiration*, *discomfort*, *pride*, and so on).

Fact and Opinion

A **fact** is a statement that you can prove through evidence.

An **opinion** is a statement that represents your belief or judgment, but which you cannot yet prove.

A. Each sentence below contains a fact and an opinion. Put one line under the fact and two lines under the opinion.

1. John bought a new car which he thinks is the best car ever made.
2. Because she felt that she might get a lot of attention, Peg joined the basketball team.
3. Darren and Hank bravely walked into the forest which everyone believed was haunted.
4. "You surely have the most beautiful house in town," Lila said when she came to visit Judy.
5. When the class judged the pictures, most of the students thought Art's drawing was the best.
6. The grocery store has several new clerks who the manager thinks will do very well.

B. Write **F** before each fact and **O** before each opinion.

O 1. Most airplane crashes seem to be the fault of careless traffic controllers.

F 2. The process of filling a rubber tire with compressed air was invented in 1888.

F 3. Several countries claim ownership of land near the South Pole.

O 4. We have the greatest baseball team ever!

O 5. I think that plants have emotions and feelings.

Name ______________________________

Teacher Note

After pupils have completed the page, stress that the word *fact* should be used only for matters that can be verified through measurement, statistical surveys, scientific observation, or direct experience. Ask pupils to explain how each sentence or sentence part they have identified as a *fact* can be verified.

Fact and Opinion

One week last summer, Lisa and Mimi visited their friend Meredith, who lives on a ranch. After the girls returned to their home in the city, they told their parents about the trip. Read the girls' statements below. Write **Fact** before each statement of fact. Write **Opinion** before each opinion.

fact 1. "The ranch house was red brick with white trim," said Lisa.

fact 2. "We watched the cowhands brand some calves," Mimi recalled.

opinion 3. "It seems to me that Meredith's family needs more help around the ranch," stated Lisa.

opinion 4. "I think ranch food is much better than the food we eat at home," announced Mimi.

fact 5. "Meredith's family took us to see a rodeo," said Lisa.

opinion 6. "A rodeo is the most exciting sport in the world to watch!" exclaimed Mimi.

opinion 7. "That was the best vacation I'll ever have for the rest of my life!" announced Lisa.

opinion 8. "I'm definitely going to work on a ranch when I grow up," said Mimi.

opinion 9. "I have a feeling that Meredith's family will invite us back again sometime," said Lisa.

fact 10. "I've already written and thanked them for showing us such a fine time," said Mimi.

Name ______________________

Teacher Note
Have pupils explain how each factual statement could be proved. For each *opinion*, have pupils suggest other opinions different people might have on the same subject.

Definition and Example

A. A **definition** of a word tells the meaning of that word. An **example** gives an illustration of a word. For each word below, choose the best definition and place its letter on the top line. Place the letter of the examples on the bottom line. The first one is done for you.

Word	Answer		Choice
1. animal	I	**A**	pepper, cloves, ginger, nutmeg
	C	**B**	a structure with four walls, a roof, and a floor
2. country	J	**C**	cows, sheep, and oxen
	G	**D**	a large stream of water
		E	school, store, home
3. building	B	**F**	Amazon, Mississippi, Nile
	E	**G**	Canada, Mexico, Italy, Spain
4. river	D	**H**	a flavored or scented plant substance
	F	**I**	any living organism that is not a plant
5. spice	H	**J**	the region of a nation or a state
	A		

B. Find the definition of each of these words in a dictionary. Write the definition on the line after **definition**. If the dictionary gives examples, write them on the line after **examples**.

1. **container** definition: Answers will vary according to the dictionaries used.

   examples: ______

2. **fern** definition: ______

   examples: ______

3. **cat** definition: ______

   examples: ______

Name ______

Teacher Note
After pupils have completed the activities, reinforce the concept of *examples* by having them suggest additional examples for the items on this page. You can also reinforce classification skills by asking pupils to classify the examples. For example, after pupils have provided examples of rivers, ask them to categorize the rivers by location.

Definition and Example

A **definition** is the meaning of a word. An **example** is the name of an item that illustrates the word. For each missing word below, a definition and some examples are given. Write **D** before each definition and **E** before each group of examples. Then, unscramble the letters printed in color to find the word being defined. Write that word on the line at the right. The first one is done for you.

1. D outerwear made of cloth
   E hat coat gloves — clothes

2. D something to sit on
   E chair bench stool — seat

3. E vine tree tulip grass — plant
   D a living thing that is not an animal

4. D something that covers or protects
   E house tent shed lean-to roof — shelter

5. D any of a group of warm-blooded vertebrates with wings
   E wren robin starling duck — bird

6. D any implement used to do work
   E hoe pliers hatchet shovel — tool

7. D the condition of the atmosphere
   E wet windy calm stormy hot breezy — weather

8. E nervous joyful tense moody giddy — emotion
   D a strong feeling

Name ______________________

Teacher Note
After pupils have completed the page, have them suggest other examples for each definition given.

A **summary** is a statement that briefly gives the main idea of a longer selection.

A. Read the paragraph and the three summaries that follow it. Underline the summary that best explains the main idea of the article. Then explain why you chose that particular summary.

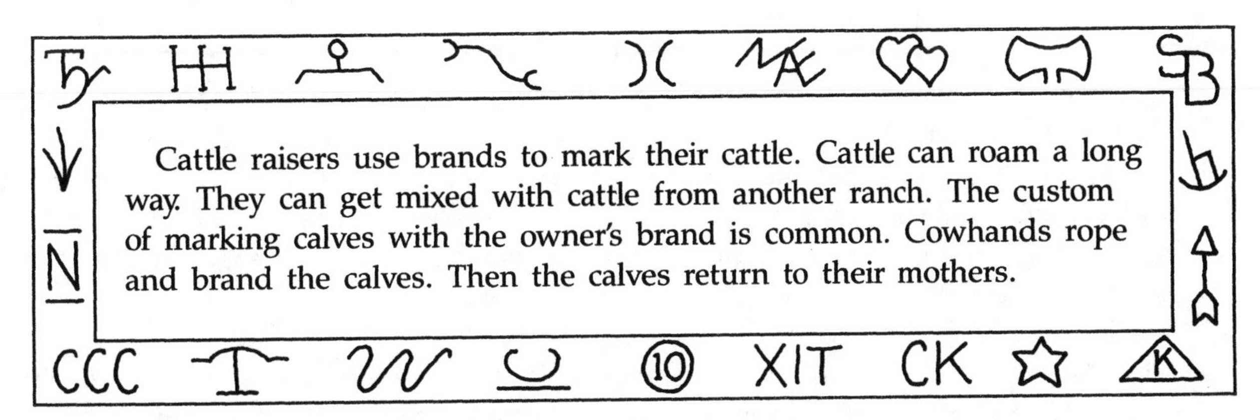

Cattle raisers use brands to mark their cattle. Cattle can roam a long way. They can get mixed with cattle from another ranch. The custom of marking calves with the owner's brand is common. Cowhands rope and brand the calves. Then the calves return to their mothers.

Summary 1. Branding cattle is not a very kind way to treat animals.

Summary 2. <u>Ranchers brand cattle so that they will not lose the animals.</u>

Summary 3. Many kinds of brands are used by ranchers. These brands help to find lost calves.

Answers will vary. Suggestion: Summary 2 gives the main idea of the entire paragraph.

Summary 1 is an opinion. Summary 3 tells only about certain details of the paragraph.

B. Read the paragraph below. Then write a summary of it.

Cellulose is the woody part of plants that gives them stiffness. Without cellulose, people would be without thousands of articles they use every day. Cotton fibers, linen cloth, coco matting, and manila rope are largely cellulose. Wood, too, is mostly cellulose, as is the paper that is made from wood. Cellulose is also used in the manufacture of certain plastics.

Answers will vary, but each should be briefer than the paragraph above.

Name

Teacher Note
After pupils have completed the activities, have them share their summaries in part B. Ask pupils what they feel are the qualities of a good summary. Pupils may benefit from pooling their various ideas to come up with a group-written summary of the paragraph.

Outlining and Summarizing

An **outline** helps you organize and remember the main idea and the details that support the main idea.

A. Read the two paragraphs below. The main idea for each is given. Fill in the details that support each main idea.

The Confrontation

Detective Yoshi gasped in disbelief as he entered the room. Every drawer in the desk was overturned; the contents lay all over the floor. The lamps from each table were smashed, and the tables were upended. Each cushion on the couch was slashed; the insides had been yanked out. The closet door was off its hinges; and shirts, socks, and sweaters hung from the shelves and lay in heaps on the floor. Even the wastebaskets had been dumped and searched.

Detective Yoshi tiptoed to the window and peered out into the street below. There in the darkness, a limousine waited, its motor running. Inside, two burly men were talking quietly. A large box was between them. As the town clock sounded, the men leaned back and looked toward the window. The detective quietly stepped back.

I. A ransacked room Probable responses:

A. Overturned drawers

B. Smashed lamps

C. Upended tables

D. Slashed cushions

E. Closet emptied

F. Wastebaskets turned over

II. A waiting limousine

A. Two burly men inside

B. A large box between them

B. Plan an ending to the story. What would happen if the men and the detective had a confrontation? Use another sheet of paper to outline your thoughts.

Name ______________________

Teacher Note
After pupils have completed the activities, have them suggest various reasons why making an outline might be a useful first step for an author.

Use the facts in this article to fill in the outline below.

General reference maps give information about where things are located, which routes are available to travelers, and the distance from one point to another. One kind of general reference map is a road map. Road maps are used by car, bus, and truck drivers. Another kind is the charts used by ship captains and airplane pilots. A globe is also a general reference map. Its map is printed onto a ball to give a truer picture of the earth's surface. A book of general reference maps is called an atlas.

Special maps show one or more important details. A weather map showing rainfall is a special map. A physical map is a special map which shows the rise and fall of land and water. A political map is a special map which uses a different color for each country.

Main Kinds of Maps

I. General reference maps

A. Road maps

B. Charts

C. Globe

D. Atlas

II. Special maps

A. Weather map

B. Physical map

C. Political map

Name ______________________

Teacher Note
After pupils have completed the page, ask them to suggest ways in which the making of an outline might be useful to a student who is preparing a social studies report.

Read the following article to find out about four kinds of animals. Then fill in the outline, telling what each animal **does** and what it **symbolizes**.

Animals and What They Symbolize

People have always enjoyed comparing animal activity to human behavior. As a result, animals have come to stand for certain things. The bee, for example, works continuously, producing honey and helping flowers grow. People, therefore, feel that the bee stands for hard work.

Spiders suck blood from the insects they trap in their webs. For this reason, spiders have become symbols of misers—people who become wealthy at the expense of others. Another animal, the snail, has come to symbolize laziness, because it moves so slowly.

The butterfly symbolizes the process of life itself. This is because butterflies go through four complete changes in their life cycle—from egg, to caterpillar, to chrysalis, to full-grown butterfly.

Suggested Answers:

Outline

I. The bee

A. Produces honey and helps flowers grow

B. Symbolizes hard work

II. The spider

A. Traps insects and sucks blood

B. Symbolizes misers

III. The snail

A. Moves slowly

B. Symbolizes laziness

IV. The butterfly

A. Changes its form

B. Symbolizes the process of life

Name ______________________________

Teacher Note
After pupils have completed the activity and shared their results, discuss the similarities among *outlining*, *classifying*, and *discriminating between definition and example*. (In all three thinking processes, the major, or general, idea is given first; under the major idea, examples are listed.)

A. Definition and Example

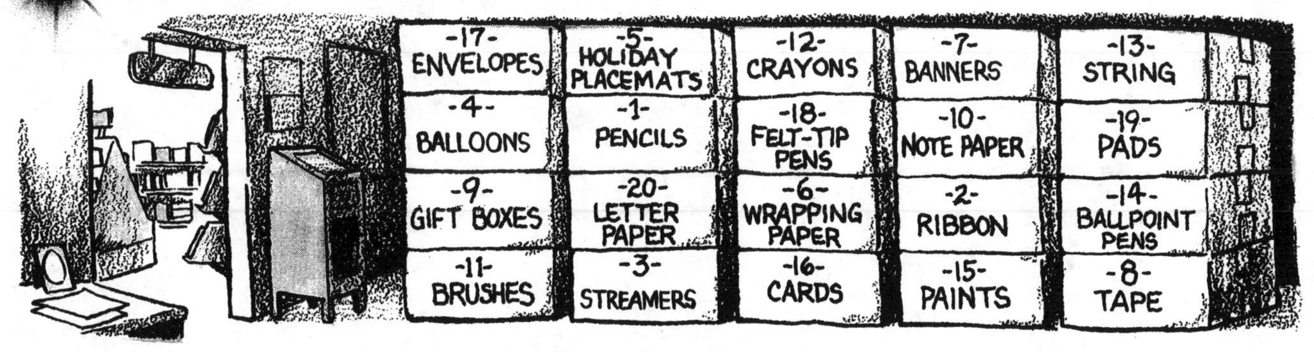

The picture above shows 20 boxes of supplies delivered to a small shop. After each definition below, write the numbers of the boxes that hold examples of the item defined. Some numbers may be placed after more than one definition.

1. **stationery**: material to be written on 17, 10, 19, 20, 16
2. **writing tools**: materials with which marks are made 12, 1, 18, 14, 11, 15
3. **decorations**: materials used as ornaments 5, 7, 4, 3
4. **packaging**: materials used to enclose, wrap, or bundle items 13, 9, 6, 2, 8

B. Outlining

Use your completed activity A above to make an outline of supplies delivered to the store.

Main topics of outline should be:

I. Stationery

II. Writing tools

III. Decorations

IV. Packaging

Details, lettered A., B., etc., should be drawn from the labels shown in the picture.

Name ______________________

Teacher Note
After completing the page, pupils may discuss and check their work with you or with a partner.

C. Real and Fanciful

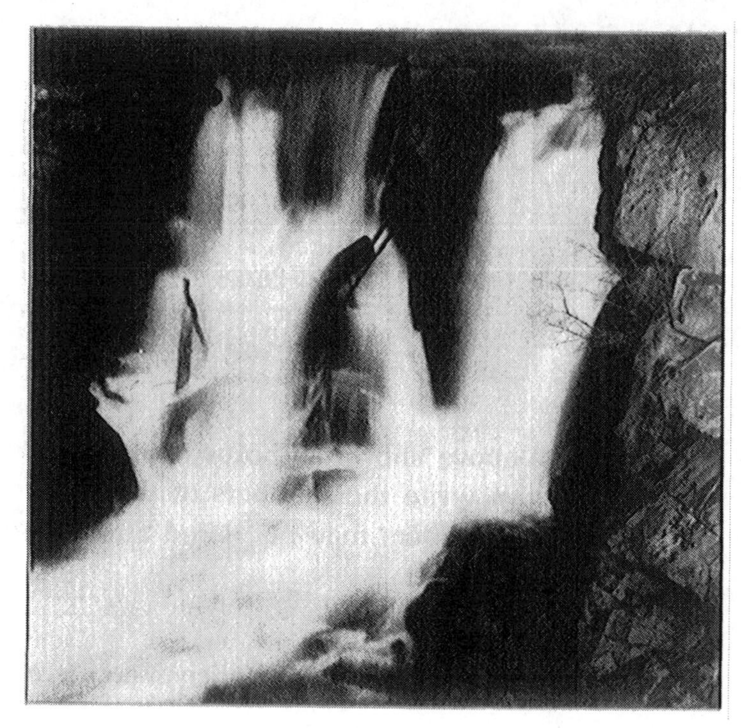

1. In the following paragraph, a writer described **dew**. To help readers picture the dew, the writer used fanciful comparisons. As you read the description, underline the comparisons.

   Little drops of dew sparkle like diamonds as they roll down the power lines like marbles. As the sun rises, the drops blink like traffic lights as they sway on the lines with the early morning breeze.

2. Study the photo of the raging waterfall. Use fanciful comparisons to write a paragraph that describes the waterfall.

   Paragraphs will vary.

D. Fact and Opinion

1. Write a sentence that states a fact about the waterfall. Sentences will vary.

2. Write a sentence that states your opinion about the waterfall.

Name

Teacher Note
After completing the page, pupils may discuss and check their work with you or with a partner.

UNIT 2

Understanding

Teacher Note

In order to develop Bloom's second stage—understanding—the pupil needs to engage in the following skills:

- Comparing and Contrasting
- Identifying Structure
- Identifying Steps in a Process
- Understanding Figural Relationships
- Comparing Word Meanings
- Identifying Main Ideas
- Identifying Relationships

Understanding means telling about something in your own words. Look at the picture. What are the girls doing? Do you think they are working independently or as a team? Have you ever worked on a group project? What was it like?

Comparing and Contrasting

To **compare** means to identify **likenesses**. To **contrast** means to identify **differences**.

Mallard Duck **Blue Jay**

A. Study the birds shown in the picture.

1. Compare the birds by listing two ways in which they are alike.

   a. Answers will vary. Possible answers: They both have wings.

   b. They both have beaks.

2. Contrast the birds by listing two ways in which they are different.

   a. They are different sizes.

   b. One is a water bird and the other is not.

B. Read the following paragraph. Then list two ways in which the hornbill and the mallee fowl are alike and two ways in which they are different.

The African hornbill and the Australian mallee fowl have unusual nest-building habits. The mallee's nest is built of many layers, with each egg resting on a different layer. The hornbill's nest has hardened mud walls. Within these nests, the eggs incubate—the mallee eggs for about seven weeks, and the hornbill eggs for five.

After the two kinds of chicks hatch, both must dig through barriers. The mallee chick must dig through the layers of the nest to the top. The hornbill chick must peck through the hard mud walls to escape.

Likenesses	**Differences**
1. Unusual nests	1. Nests made differently
2. Chicks dig through barriers	2. Different incubation time

Name ______________________

Teacher Note
After pupils have completed the page, discuss other ways in which the birds in both the picture and the paragraph might be compared and contrasted. Ascertain that pupils know the difference in meaning between the words *compare* and *contrast*.

Comparing and Contrasting

A. Each sentence group below **compares** two things, or shows how they are alike. On the line after each group, write a sentence which **contrasts** the things, or shows how they are different.

Answers will vary.

1. A chair and a bed are both furniture. They both have four legs. ____________

2. An auditorium is designed for recreation, as is a gymnasium. Both are large and hold many people. ____________

3. Pins and needles are both used for sewing. They are small, sharp objects meant to hold material together. ____________

4. Soccer and football are both team sports involving the use of a ball. Players attempt to move the ball toward a goal. ____________

5. Diamonds and iron are both hard. Both must be brought out from mines. ____________

B. For each pair of items below, write a sentence to tell how the items are alike.

1. A tractor and a pair of roller skates Answers will vary. ____________

2. A tree and an umbrella ____________

3. A diary and a telephone ____________

4. A guitar and a bird ____________

Name ____________

Teacher Note
After pupils have completed part A, have them compare and contrast their responses—that is, tell which answers are alike and which are different. As pupils undertake part B, encourage them to use their imaginations. In sharing their responses to this activity, pupils will grow in their ability to make metaphors and use divergent thinking.

Comparing and Contrasting

Read the following description of a **hobbit**. Then, at the bottom of the page, write a paragraph in which you both compare and contrast yourself to one of these fanciful creatures.

I suppose hobbits need some description nowadays, since they have become rare and shy of the Big People, as they call us. They are (or were) a little people, about half our height, and smaller than the bearded Dwarves. Hobbits have no beards. There is little or no magic about them, except the ordinary everyday sort which helps them to disappear quietly and quickly when large stupid folk like you and me come blundering along, making a noise like elephants which they can hear a mile off. They are inclined to be fat in the stomach; they dress in bright colours (chiefly green and yellow); wear no shoes, because their feet grow natural leathery soles and thick warm brown hair like the stuff on their heads (which is curly); have long clever brown fingers, good-natured faces, and laugh deep fruity laughs (especially after dinner, which they have twice a day when they can get it).

— from *The Hobbit* by J.R.R. Tolkien

Answers will vary.

Name

Teacher Note
Have pupils share and discuss their responses. Encourage them to take delight in the various and different comparisons and contrasts that result from the writing activity.

Identifying Structure

A **cinquain** is a special kind of five-line poem. A cinquain may follow either of the forms, or structures, described on this page.

A. Study the cinquain at the bottom of the page. Decide which structure it follows. Then copy the cinquain on the five lines next to that structure.

B. On the remaining five lines, write your own cinquain, following the cinquain structure next to it.

Structure I

Line 1: one noun stating the subject — Poems will vary in subject matter, but all should adhere to Structure I. ____________

Line 2: two adjectives describing the noun ____________

Line 3: three action verbs ____________

Line 4: four words showing feeling about the subject ____________

Line 5: another word for the word in Line 1 ____________

Structure II

Line 1: two syllables naming the subject — My hat

Line 2: four syllables describing the subject — Fuzzy, warm, soft

Line 3: six syllables showing action — Protects, covers, cuddles

Line 4: eight syllables showing feeling about the subject — Makes a whirl of color on snow

Line 5: two syllables that stand for the word or words in Line 1 — Ski cap

My hat
Fuzzy, warm, soft
Protects, covers, cuddles
Makes a whirl of color on snow
Ski cap

Name ____________

Teacher Note
Encourage pupils to check each other's cinquains to make sure they follow Structure I. Then discuss pupils' feelings about writing a poem to adhere to a certain pattern. Have them name other poetry structures that they may be familiar with, such as jingles, couplets, and limericks. Ask pupils whether they prefer writing poetry to a pattern or in a free form.

SKILL 7 Identifying Structure

Letters make up the structure of a written word. In the word games below, you will play with the structure of words to form other words. In both games, you will be forming **synonyms**, or words that have almost the same meaning.

A. In each word pair below, take a letter from the top word and place it in the bottom word to make a pair of synonyms. Keep the letters of the bottom word in the same order. The first pair has been done for you.

1. leash	lash	3. boast	boat	5. turns	turn
bat	beat	hip	ship	pin	spin
2. stalk	talk	4. furry	fury	6. quiet	quit
peak	speak	age	rage	lave	leave

B. Change the order of the letters in both words of each pair below to form pairs of synonyms. The first pair has been done for you.

1. cork	rock	4. heat	hate	8. peels	sleep
notes	stone	tested	detest	pan	nap
2. strut	trust	5. paws	swap	9. fare	fear
lyre	rely	tread	trade	dared	dread
3. stop	spot	6. carve	crave	10. least	steal
saint	stain	reside	desire	orb	rob
		7. leap	peal		
		grin	ring		

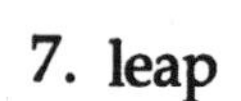

Name ______________________________

Teacher Note
Discuss with pupils other word games in which a structure must be adhered to (crossword puzzles, word searches, certain board games, and so on). Have pupils determine whether it would be possible to play a game that had *no* structure. Ask what a structureless game would be like.

Steps in a Process

A. The pictures below make a cartoon. They are similar to a filmstrip. On the lines below the pictures, write what you think is happening in each picture.

1. Answers will vary but should tell the story in sequence.
2. ______
3. ______
4. ______
5. ______
6. ______

B. In which picture is humor first introduced? 4 Why is it humorous? A police officer would not tell a cat about a traffic sign.

C. Is this a real or fanciful situation? fanciful

Why? It would not really happen.

Name ______

Teacher Note
After pupils have completed the page and discussed their responses, explain that writers often begin their thinking by planning what will happen at the end of the story. Once they have decided on an ending, they must identify the steps that the characters will follow in order to reach this ending. Pupils might enjoy working in groups to write stories following this method.

Steps in a Process

Read the paragraphs below to learn the steps used to make maple syrup. On the lines below the paragraphs, use your own words to tell the steps in order. There are six steps. The first one is given to help you get started.

Maple syrup is made from the sap of sugar maple trees. These trees are found in the northeastern United States and in Canada. To collect the sap, farmers bore holes into the tree trunks about four feet from the ground. Small metal or plastic spouts are forced into the holes. Buckets are hung from the spouts to collect sap as it flows from the holes.

The sap is poured into large tanks and is moved by sleds to a sap house. There a machine called an evaporator boils the sap until some of the water has evaporated. The remaining liquid is maple syrup.

1. Bore holes into tree trunks.
2. Probable responses: Force spouts into the holes.
3. Hang buckets from spouts to collect sap.
4. Pour sap into large tanks.
5. Take tanks to sap house.
6. Boil sap.

Name ______________________

Teacher Note
After pupils have completed the page, discuss occasions when it is important to list or understand the steps in any process, for example, in following directions for making something or for playing a game. Encourage pupils to use the word *understand* as they talk about sequential steps and their relationship to general ideas.

Figural Relationships

Figure and **figural** are words that refer to such things as charts, diagrams, and symbols. Such figures can help you see and understand quickly how facts are related.

A. Study the **bar graph** below. Then complete the sentences that follow it.

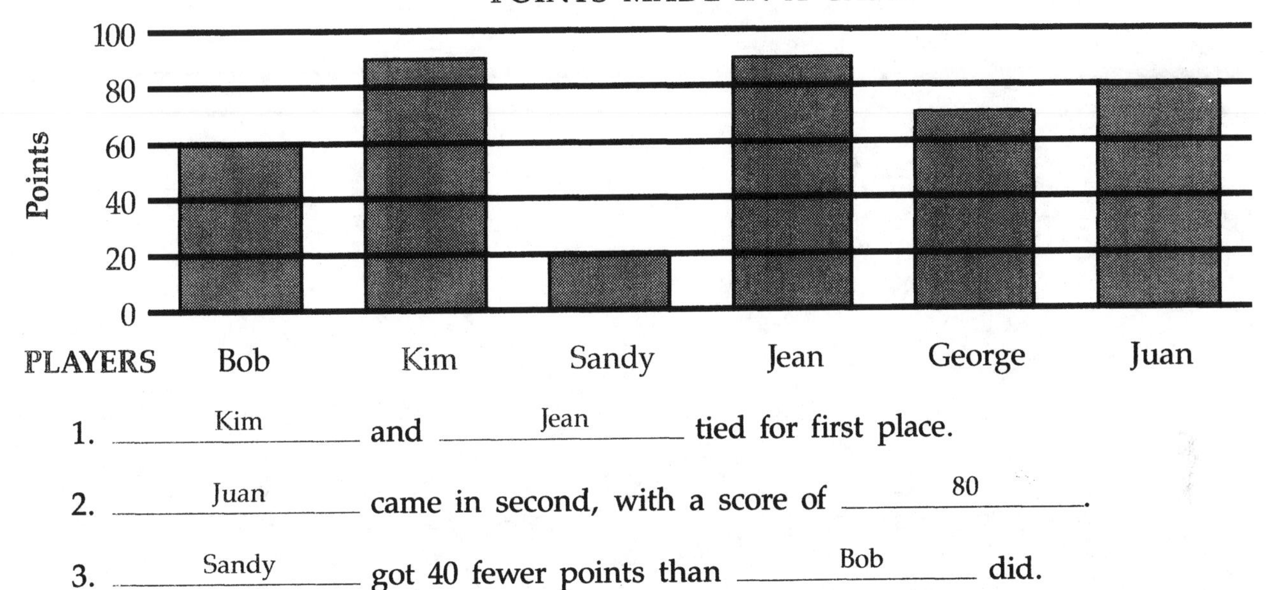

1. Kim and Jean tied for first place.

2. Juan came in second, with a score of 80.

3. Sandy got 40 fewer points than Bob did.

B. The **line graph** below shows George's scores for six different games. Study the graph. Then complete the sentences and answer the question that follows.

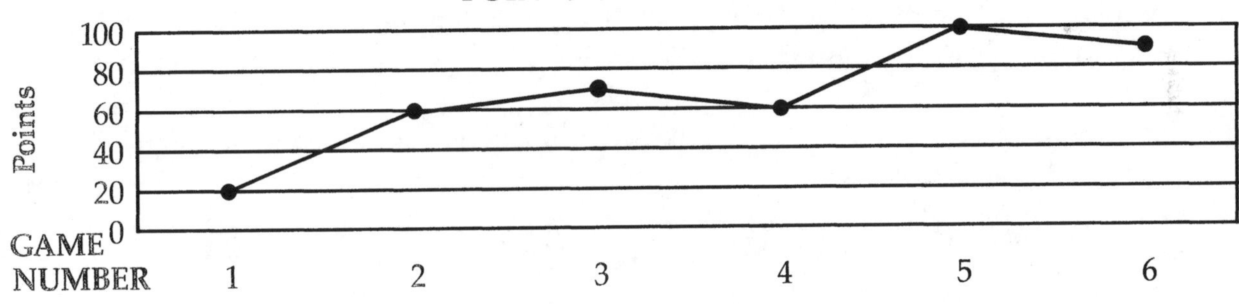

1. George got his highest score in game 5.

2. The first time he played, George's score was 20.

3. George's scores were the same in games 2 and 4.

4. In general, did George improve, get worse, or stay about the same as he played the game? George improved as he played.

Name ______________________________

Teacher Note
Discuss with pupils the subject areas in which they are most likely to read or construct graphs, diagrams, charts, and other materials which give information in figure or picture form (social studies, science, math). Help pupils see that these figures are useful in giving an overall, fast survey of the general idea, as well as the particular facts which make up that general idea.

Figural Relationships

The figures below—with their circles, letters, and colors—make up what is called a **three-circle code**. The **key** below the code shows the symbols that can be used for the letters in the first circle.

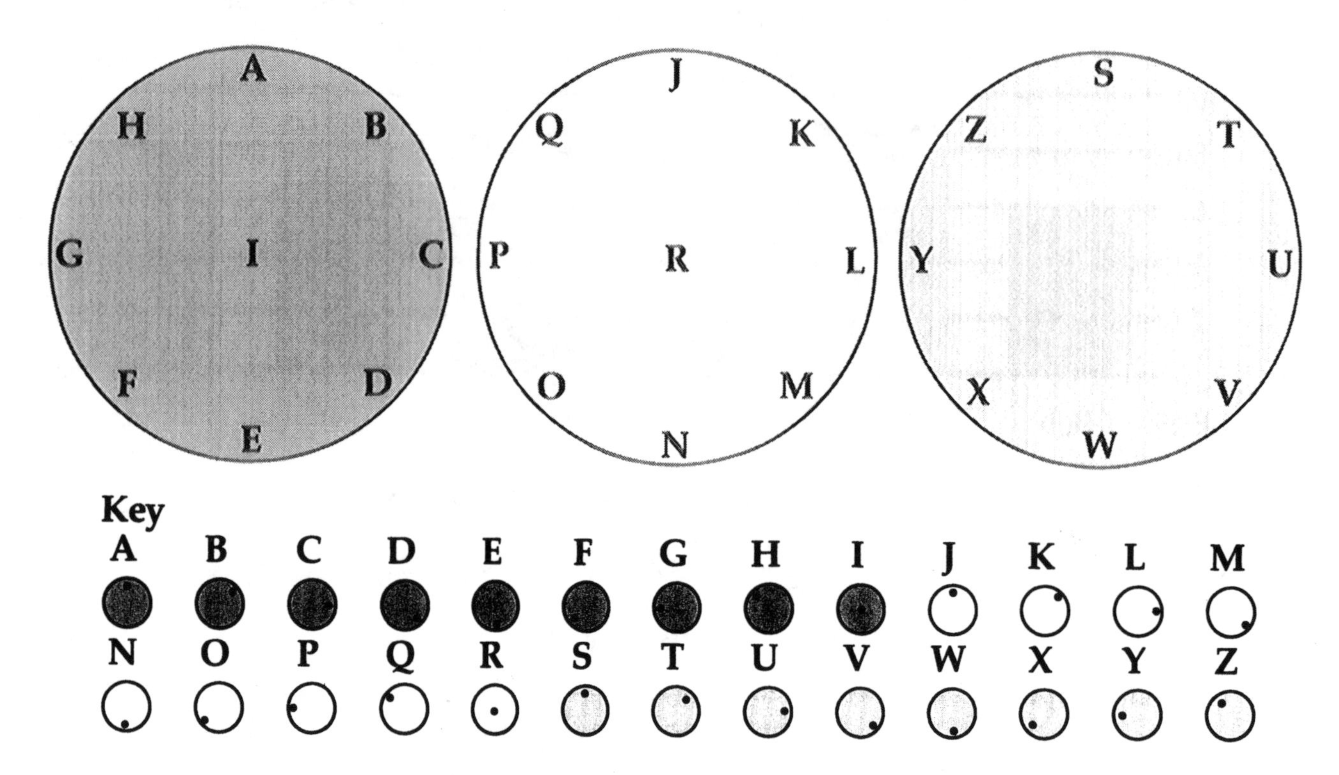

A. Complete the Key to show the symbols for the letters in the second and third circles. Use a pencil—lightly—to indicate the gray color used in the third circle.

B. Use a regular pencil and a colored pencil to encode the following saying: **It is better to be safe than sorry**.

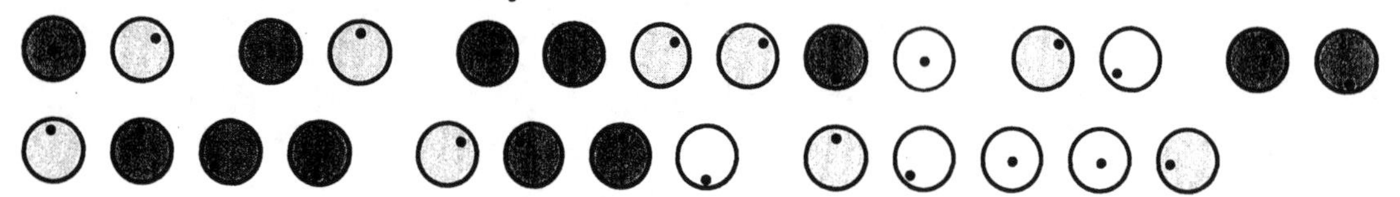

C. Decode the following to find another saying.

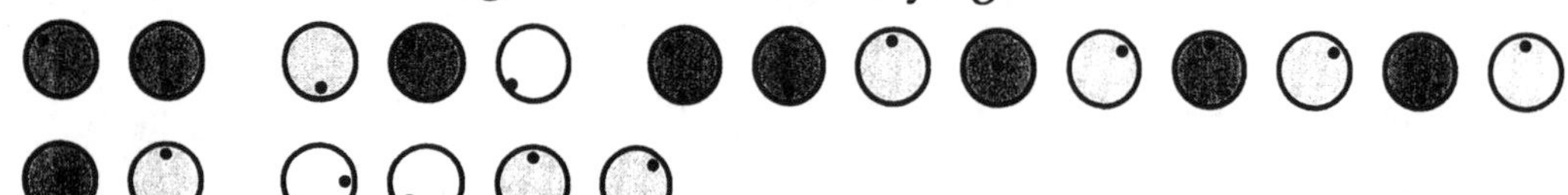

He who hesitates is lost.

Name

Teacher Note
Discuss with pupils other kinds of codes that they know about and/or have used. Have pupils determine when codes are particularly useful in real-life situations, for example, to radio messages via Morse Code, to signal from ship to ship through the use of semaphore flags, and to read through the use of Braille.

Comparing Word Meanings

Read the words in each group below. Then find the word in the **Word List** that is related to each word in the group and write it on the line. The first one is done for you.

pin	1. straight, safety, bowling, clothes, rolling
pen	2. pig, ball-point, bull, play
wheel	3. wagon, steering, potter's, ship's, spinning
ring	4. circus, boxing, tree, bathtub, telephone
shell	5. sea, egg, pie, snail
star	6. movie, general's, shooting, lucky
teeth	7. false, gear, saw, rake, comb
story	8. mystery, picture, short, news
plate	9. home, dinner, paper, license
bed	10. hospital, flower, water, rock
glass	11. spy, eye, field, drinking, window
key	12. piano, musical, lock, answer, code
table	13. multiplication, dining, time
light	14. night, flash, sun, sky
nail	15. finger, toe, roofing, finishing, six-penny

Word List

wheel
story
key
shell
pen
ring
teeth
light
pin
plate
nail
glass
bed
star
table

Name ______________________________

Teacher Note
After pupils have completed the page, discuss the meaning of each resulting term, for example, *lucky star*, *spinning wheel*, *spyglass*, and so on.

Comparing Word Meanings

Below are two games of Word Tic-Tac-Toe. In each bracket, a word is printed above the line: huge ______. Pick a synonym for the word from the list below.

Write the synonym below the word: huge ______ gigantic. The first player to complete a row of brackets across, up and down, or diagonally is the winner. Not all of the words will be used.

SYNONYM SEARCH BOX

hug
qualified
elect
mislay
tumult
miniature
radiant
rapid
reaction
ready
genuine
violin
reap
revolt
restore
remember
still
sensational
foolish
show
tremble
vanish
surprise
vague
accentuate
expire
ragged

GAME I

emphasize accentuate	embrace hug	eligible qualified
elapse expire	misplace mislay	shining radiant
choose elect	uproar tumult	tattered ragged

GAME II

swift rapid	real genuine	rebuild restore
response reaction	harvest reap	recall remember
prepared ready	rebellion revolt	thrilling sensational

Name ______________________________

Teacher Note
Pupils should work in pairs on this page. When they have finished playing the games, discuss the slight differences in meanings, even between synonyms. (It will be helpful to have dictionaries available.) Ask pupils to use each word in a sentence to show how each would be used in context.

Identifying Main Ideas

A good paragraph is built around a **main idea**. Often, this main idea is stated in a **topic sentence**. At other times, there is no topic sentence, though the facts in the paragraph are still clustered around a main idea.

A. Read each paragraph below. If the paragraph has a topic sentence, underline that sentence.

1. Water has many unusual properties. For example, a skin forms where water meets air. Tiny water droplets squeeze together and move upward through stems and leaves. Water also floats when it is frozen, because frozen water has expanded and become less dense.

2. One hero of the First World War was a pigeon that carried an important message through artillery fire. During the Second World War, the British dropped boxes of homing pigeons behind enemy lines. Pigeons were also used to carry messages during the Korean War.

3. The camel is well-equipped for desert travel. Its long eyelashes help keep the blowing sand out of its eyes. A camel can travel for several days without water. Thick pads protect its hoofs from the hot sand.

4. A hippopotamus can run on the bottom of a lake or river at eight miles an hour. On land, it can run as fast as a human. This large animal is a fast swimmer and can dive, sink like a rock, or float like a log.

5. Though insects are small, many of them can cause great damage. Some insects can destroy crops. Others can cause various illnesses in people and in other animals.

B. A good title states the main idea briefly and in an interesting way. On the following lines, write a title for each paragraph above.

1. Answers will vary but should encapsulate the main idea. ____________________

2. ____________________

3. ____________________

4. ____________________

5. ____________________

Name ____________________

Teacher Note
After pupils have completed and discussed the activities, ask them to think of everyday situations in which they see main ideas stated, as in newspaper headlines, TV news "briefs," and special sale signs in stores. You may also discuss how the identification of main ideas is useful in the construction of an outline.

Identifying Main Ideas

Read each group of sentences below. Decide which sentence seems unrelated to the others, and draw a line through it. Then think of a **main-idea**, or **topic**, sentence that could be used to introduce the remaining three sentences. Write a paragraph, using your topic sentence and following it with the three related sentences.

A. 1. Native Americans could tell direction in the forest by examining where moss grew.
   2. Broken branches and twigs were clues to the paths taken by forest animals.
   3. ~~Native Americans told a variety of myths and legends.~~
   4. Keen ears could pick up the special sounds made by different birds and mammals.

Topic sentences will vary.

B. 1. The investigations of scientists have led to the cures for many diseases.
   2. ~~Scientists hold conventions frequently.~~
   3. A scientist's patient investigations can also unfold important facts about the earth and about the universe.
   4. The results of any investigation lead to new and fascinating questions which may be answered by further study.

Topic sentences will vary.

Name

Teacher Note
Ask pupils to explain why the deleted sentences do not relate to the main ideas. Discuss the topic sentences they constructed, pointing out the strong points of each.

Identifying Relationships

Events are often related in **time**. Often, words such as **then**, **next**, or **as** are clues that let you know the time order that relates the events.

Read the sentences below and follow these three steps.

A. Circle the clue word or phrase that shows the time relationship between the events.
B. If one event happened before the other, underline the part of the sentence that tells what happened first.
C. If both events happened at the same time, put a check on the line before the sentence.

___√___ 1. When Jim drove the car into the driveway, he noticed that the garage door was open.

______ 2. He carefully eased out from under the wheel, after parking the car.

______ 3. Before he even opened the door to the house, Jim could tell that something strange was going on.

___√___ 4. As Jim entered the kitchen, he heard odd noises coming from the living room.

______ 5. He was not frightened until the noises got louder.

______ 6. He hesitated, and then walked bravely through the kitchen to the hall.

___√___ 7. Outside the living room, Jim's heart pounded while the strange noises continued.

______ 8. After deciding to look now or never, Jim yanked the door open.

___√___ 9. When he looked around, Jim was surprised to see only his father with some friends.

______ 10. Looking puzzled, Jim stepped into the room and then smiled with relief.

___√___ 11. At the same moment, Jim's father turned on some new electronic drum machines.

______ 12. After Jim's excitement was over, his father showed him how to use the drum machines.

Name ______________________________

Teacher Note
Discuss with pupils the time words they have identified. Ask them to use the same word or phrase in an original sentence.

Identifying Relationships

Events are often related because one event causes the other to happen. This is called a **cause-effect** relationship. Clue words such as **because, since**, and **as a result** often signal a cause-effect relationship.

A. Read the following paragraphs. In each blank, write a clue word or phrase which points out the cause-effect relationship between the events.

1. Before the invention of the steam engine, ships used the power of the wind to move across the seas. It took from three to four weeks to sail from America to Europe. Because or Since ______ the winds generally blew from west to east, it took longer to go from Europe to America.

2. During the last century, pioneers began to have a difficult time finding vast stretches of land in the East. As a result ______, they started to travel westward across the country in covered wagons.

3. Seashell collecting was once a popular hobby. Because or Since ______ many varieties of seashells have now become rare, ecologists are discouraging people from continuing this hobby.

B. Complete each sentence to make it show a cause-effect relationship. Answers will vary.

1. The team won the tournament because ______

______

2. Our field trip was a success because ______

______

3. Since it is beginning to snow, our trip to the mountains ______

______

4. New speed-limit laws were passed, and, as a result, ______

______

Name ______

Teacher Note
Discuss pupils' responses to both activities. For part B, ask classmates to judge whether or not the cause-effect relationship makes sense.

Identifying Relationships

The first two sentences in each group below tell about events that at first do not seem to be related to one another. The third sentence, however, tells about an event that was caused by the first two. On the lines below each word group, explain the cause-effect relationship. Answers will vary. Possible responses:

1. Mrs. Brown bought a toy in New York. Six-year-old Vivian lived in London. Vivian played with her new toy. Mrs. Brown sent the toy to Vivian.

2. Mountains near the town of Troy received heavy rainfall. In the valley some miles away was a small stream. Rather suddenly the small stream flooded. Water flowed down the mountainside into the stream.

3. Mr. and Mrs. Roberts were robbed one dark night. Jane Roberts was away at college, studying accounting. Jane began to look for a job. Jane wanted to help her parents get some money together.

4. The price of gasoline rose a great deal. Yuji works in a city several miles from his home. Yuji now rides to work with three other people. Yuji and his friends save money through a car-pool.

5. Several stores suddenly closed. The power company moved to another town. The school enrollment dropped. The town's population decreased.

Name ____________________

Teacher Note
Discuss pupils' explanatory sentences. Have them decide why or why not various sentences are sensible. Pupils may wish to revise some of their sentences after this discussion.

Identifying Relationships

Sometimes objects or ideas are related according to how they are arranged in a space. Such relationships are called **spatial relationships**. To understand a spatial relationship, you must move your eyes not only from left to right, as you do in reading, but also up and down and all around.

Study the drawings below, then do the activities that follow them.

elephant

engine

eagle

John

A. Write two sentences to tell two ways in which all the drawings are alike.

1. Each is made of letters.
2. Each shows the thing named by the word.

B. On the line below each drawing, spell out the word shown in the drawing.

C. Now use what you have learned about spatial relationships to make drawings of the following words:

cowboy

giraffe

1. escalator	2. whale	3. chain	4. (your own name)

Name ____________________

Teacher Note
Discuss pupils' responses to parts A and B. Ask pupils to share their drawings in part C. Then discuss occasions in which thinking is done visually, as in studying a painting, riding a bike or driving through the community, deciding which chore to tackle first in cleaning up a room, or observing weather conditions to determine what clothing to wear.

This photograph was taken after a marathon race. As you study the picture, imagine that you are the newspaper reporter who will write about the race.

A. Identifying Main Ideas

Write a headline to accompany the photo. Your headline should state the main idea.

Answers may vary.

____

B. Comparing and Contrasting

On the lines below, make notes comparing and contrasting the runners shown in the photograph.

How the Runners Are Alike	How the Runners Are Different
Answers will vary.	

C. Identifying Relationships

Write a caption to go with the photo. Make up names for the winner and the runners-up. Your caption should show **time relationships** with the words **first**, **next**, and **last**. You might also include a **cause-effect relationship** to explain how the winner won the race.

Answers will vary.

____

____

____

Name ____

Teacher Note
After completing the page, pupils may discuss and check their work with you or with a classmate.

Refer to the figure as you complete the following activities.

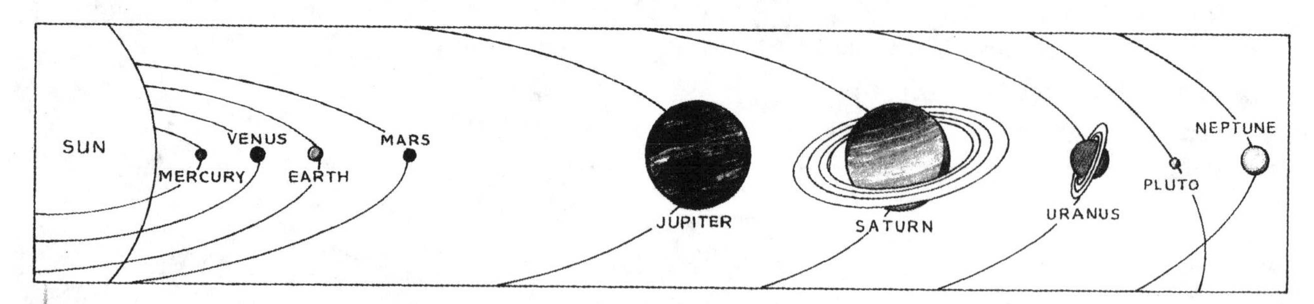

D. Figural Relationships

Which main heavenly bodies make up the solar system? Which body lies at the center of the solar system? How do the other bodies move around it?

The sun and nine planets make up the solar system.

The sun lies at the center.

The planets travel around the sun in oval-shaped paths, or orbits.

E. Comparing and Contrasting

How does the size of the planets farther from the sun compare with the size of the planets closer to it? Except for Pluto, the farther planets are much larger than the closer planets.

F. Identifying Relationships

What position from the sun is Earth? Does Earth lie between Venus and the sun, or does Venus lie between Earth and the sun? Does Pluto ever lie between Neptune and the sun?

Earth is the third planet from the sun.

Venus lies between Earth and the sun.

Sometimes Pluto moves between Neptune and the sun.

Name ____________________

Teacher Note
After completing the page, have pupils discuss their work with you or with a classmate.

UNIT 3 Applying

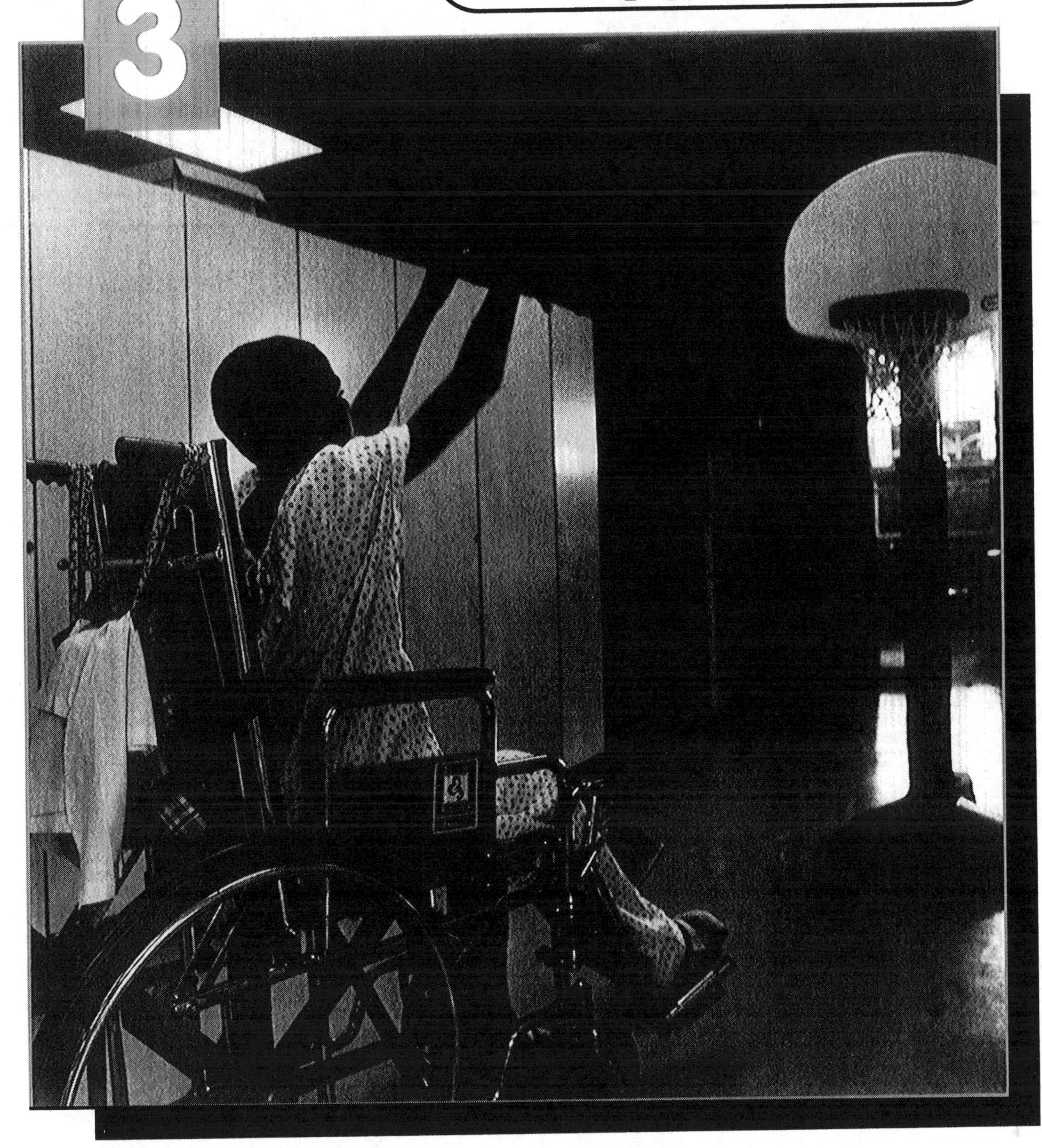

Teacher Note
In order to develop Bloom's third stage—applying—the pupil needs to engage in the following skills:
- Ordering Objects
- Estimating
- Anticipating Probabilities
- Inferring
- Interpreting Changes in Word Meanings

Applying means using what you know. Let's try it out. Look at the picture. What is the boy doing? Do you think the boy has played basketball before? Have you ever played a game that was hard to learn? What was it like once you learned how to play?

SKILL 13

Ordering Objects

Objects can be put in different **orders**, according to the standard you are using. In the activities below, you will use two different standards for ordering objects.

A. Number the words in each column from **1** to **6** according to the number of syllables each word contains.

1		2		3	
4	information	3	restriction	3	cottonwood
2	outward	6	electronically	6	automatically
1	source	2	ocean	1	cough
6	mathematically	4	invisibly	2	fiddle
3	photograph	1	fair	4	grammatical
5	organization	5	superintendent	5	metropolitan

B. Arrange the figures below in order according to the size of the shaded parts. Write **1** on the line below the figure with smallest shaded part and continue numbering until the largest part is numbered **8**.

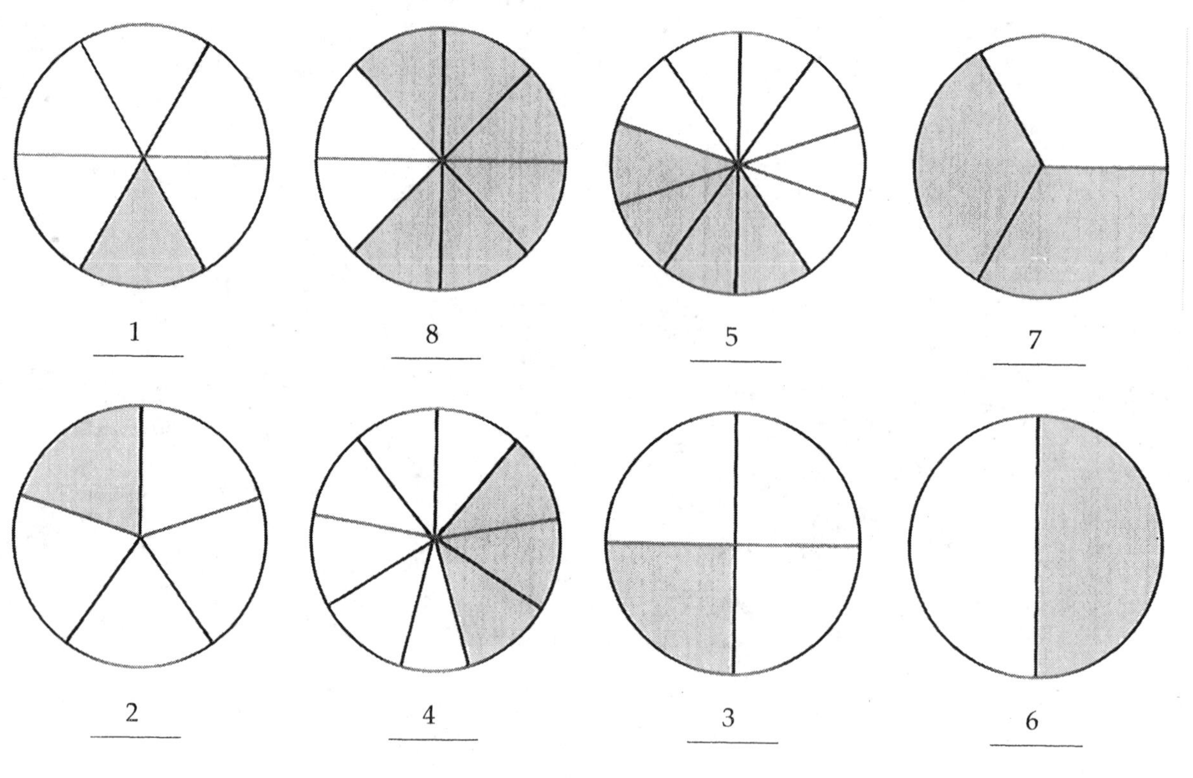

Name ______________________________

Teacher Note
After pupils have completed the page, discuss the skills they used as they completed each exercise. (In part A, pupils applied what they know about determining the number of syllables in a word. In part B, pupils applied their visual knowledge.)

Ordering Objects

A. Number each column of objects from the thinnest to the thickest. Write **1** before the thinnest. Continue until the thickest is labeled **3**. The first column is done for you.

1		**2**		**3**	
2	pamphlet	3	rope	2	branch
3	book	2	string	3	trunk
1	paper	1	thread	1	twig

B. In the groups below, order the objects according to weight. Use **1** for the lightest, **3** for the heaviest, and **2** for the object that is in between.

2	dog	2	quart	3	ton
1	mouse	1	pint	1	gram
3	elephant	3	gallon	2	kilogram

C. Think of two different standards you could use to order the objects at the bottom of the page. Then write the different standards on the column-heading lines and list the objects. Answers will vary. Examples are given.

Standard 1: Size	Standard 2: Number of Wheels
roller skate	wheelbarrow
wheelbarrow	bicycle
bicycle	roller skate
tractor-trailer	tractor-trailer

Name ______________________________

Teacher Note
After pupils have completed the page, discuss their responses in parts A and B. Then ask pupils to explain the standards and ordering systems they used in part C.

Ordering Objects

A. List the products below according to their importance to human life, their cost, and their durability (how long they last).

television, bread, car, bed, house, piano, light bulb

1 Most important first	2 Most expensive first	3 Longest lasting first
Answers will vary.	house	house
	car or piano	television, car, bed, or piano
	car or piano	may be listed in varying orders
	bed or television	
	bed or television	
	light bulb or bread	light bulb
	light bulb or bread	bread

B. List some animals that are useful to humans and explain the uses. When your list is complete, number from the most useful animal to the least. Answers will vary.

Animal	Uses

Name

Teacher Note
Discuss with pupils which listings are based on a fact, and which are based on opinion. Ask pupils to explain why they ordered the objects a particular way.

Estimating

An **estimate** is a rough judgment about how long or large something is or about how long it will take to accomplish a task. While an estimate is not exact, it is somewhat more reliable than a **guess**. That is because an estimate is based on some kind of standard, such as a picture, a scale, a key, or your own experience.

Study the map of the United States and the key. Then on the chart below the map, write your estimates of the distance between the various cities shown on the map. An estimate of the distance between Miami and Seattle has already been given to help you get started.

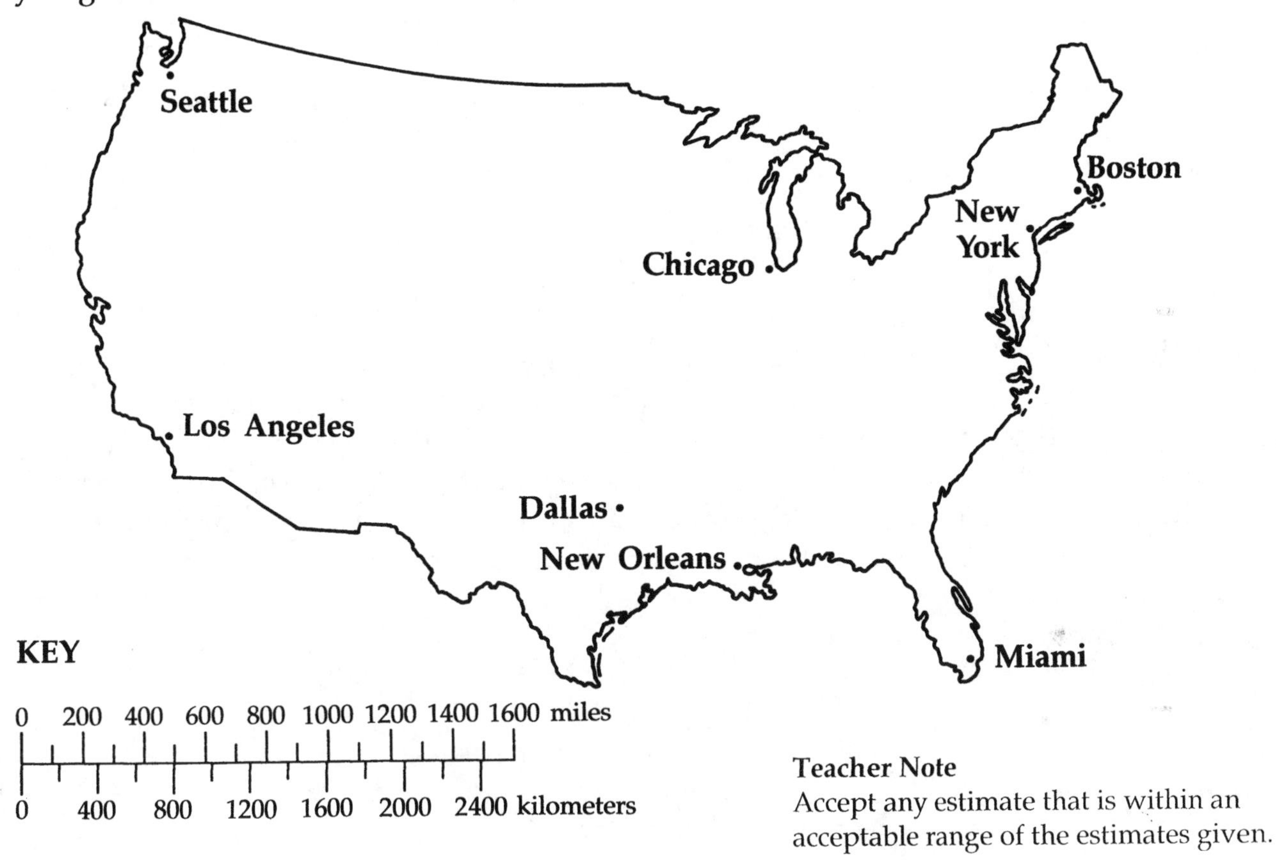

Teacher Note
Accept any estimate that is within an acceptable range of the estimates given.

	Boston	New Orleans	Chicago	Seattle
New York	200 mi (325 km)	1400 mi (2250 km)	875 mi (1400 km)	2850 mi (4600 km)
Miami	1500 mi (2400 km)	850 mi (1300 km)	1375 mi (2200 km)	3200 mi (5100 km)
Los Angeles	3300 mi (5300 km)	1900 mi (3100 km)	1800 mi (2900 km)	1125 mi (1800 km)
Dallas	1800 mi (2900 km)	450 mi (700 km)	900 mi (1450 km)	2000 mi (3200 km)

Name ____________________

Teacher Note
After pupils have completed and compared their mileage and made any corrections they wish, discuss with them where and how they would gather the exact information regarding distances between cities. As pupils undertake this analysis, have them consider the difference between air distance and distance when traveling over land and why the difference exists.

Estimating

A. Estimate the amount of time it would take **you**—working at the top of your form—to do each of the following chores: Answers will vary.

1. paint a gate for your fence ______
2. wash breakfast dishes for a family of four ______
3. buy a three-day supply of groceries ______
4. read 20 pages in a history book ______
5. clean out a small aquarium ______
6. write a composition about autumn ______
7. clean out your desk ______

B. Now imagine that you have been asked to do all the tasks listed above in a single day. On the chart below, make a schedule. In the right-hand column, list the chores in the order in which you would prefer to do them. In the column at the left, show as closely as possible—in hours and minutes—when you would begin the task and when you would probably finish it. For example, you might write 8 A.M. — 8:30 A.M. to show the time span for doing a chore. Answers will vary.

TIME	CHORE
______	______
______	______
______	______
______	______
______	______
______	______
______	______

Name ______

Teacher Note
Discuss with pupils why answers will vary in these activities. Help pupils to see that some estimates must be made on the basis of an individual's knowledge of how fast he or she worked on a similar task in the past and on the application of one's knowledge about which tasks one prefers to do first, next, and so forth.

Anticipating Probabilities

A **probability** is something that is very likely to happen. For example, if you do not water a plant for a long time, it is **probable** that the plant will die.

A. Complete each sentence below by telling what the **probable** outcome will be.
Answers will vary. Possibilities are given.

1. If it does not rain for some time, it is probable that
a water shortage will be declared.

2. If the school band practices hard every day, it is probable that the band concert
will be a success.

3. If a player throws a ball at the basketball hoop 100 times, it is probable that
the player will often get the ball through the hoop.

4. If you forget to bring your lunch to school, it is probable that
you will go hungry.

5. If you manage to save one dollar every week, it is probable that you will be able
to save enough money to buy something important.

B. A situation may have more than one probable outcome. Read about the situations below. Then list two probable outcomes for each situation. Answers will vary. Possibilities are given.

1. Mary and Ian are scheduled to play a piano duet on Friday. They are both excellent players, but they have practiced very little together. Mary and Ian will probably
   a. schedule some practice time together.
   b. do well in their duet.

2. Leon is very shy. He has worked very hard to learn Spanish. As a result, he has been offered a chance to live with a family in Latin America this summer, along with students from other schools who have done well in Spanish. Leon will probably
   a. overcome his fears and go on the trip.
   b. ask to stay with someone he knows.

Name ______________________

Teacher Note
After pupils have completed the page, discuss their reasons for deciding each *probable* outcome.

Anticipating Probabilities

You know that a **probability** is something that is very likely to happen. A **possibility**, on the other hand, is something that **might** or **could** happen if certain other conditions happened, too.

A. Read each sentence below. Then write **probability** or **possibility** on the line before the sentence.

1. probability This week, someone in your class will get a score of 90 or above on a paper or test.
2. probability This winter, areas of the Northeast will get heavy snowfalls and high winds.
3. possibility This year, a severe earthquake will hit the area in which you live.
4. possibility Within the next ten years, intelligent beings from another galaxy will visit Earth.
5. possibility Within the next ten years, all the nations of the Western Hemisphere will unite to form one nation.

B. Select two of the sentences in part A which you have labeled **possible**. On the lines below, tell what you would **probably** do or how your life would **probably** change, if such an event actually happened.

1. Answers will vary.

2.

Name

Teacher Note
Discuss with pupils their reasons for labeling each sentence in part A *possiblility* or *problablility*. Have pupils share their responses to part B. Then discuss ways in which a writer of fantasy or science fiction uses the concepts of *probability* and *possibility* in constructing a story.

Inferring

To **infer** means to reach a conclusion based on what you observe or the facts you have at hand.

Study the picture of the house. Examine the details carefully. Then write a paragraph to tell what you **infer** about the house. For example, do you infer that the house is empty or occupied? Do you infer that people in the neighborhood like or dislike this particular house? For each inference that you make, give at least one picture-detail that has led you to that inference.

Answers will vary.

Name

Teacher Note
Discuss with pupils the different inferences they have made. List them on the chalkboard.

Inferring

Many times, an inference is correct. You have enough facts at hand to lead you logically to the correct conclusion. At other times, however, an inference may **not** be correct. As you gather additional information, your inference may change. You may come to a different conclusion.

Here are some facts that may lead you to change your inference about the house you studied on page 49:

- The owner, Mr. M., is old and ill.
- Mr. M.'s wife and other close relatives died sometime ago.
- Mr. M. is extremely shy.
- Mr. M. has very little money.

1. On the basis of the facts above, write a few sentences which explain the condition of the house shown in the picture on page 49.

   Answers will vary but should take the facts above into account.

2. On the basis of the facts above, what would you infer about the kinds of things that Mr. M. needs most?

   Answers will vary. Possibilities: friendship, a source of income, help from neighbors to get his house in order.

3. In many cases, it is important to check further to make sure an inference is correct. How would you check to see whether the inference you made in number 2 is correct?

   Answers will vary. Possibilities: Ask Mr. M. Ask a social worker. Discuss the situation with neighbors.

Name ______________________

Teacher Note
Discuss with pupils why our first inferences may not be entirely correct. Discuss why the pupils' inferences about the old house changed as additional facts about it were given. Have pupils discuss and compare their responses to number 3 and decide which suggested procedures would be the best ones to take.

Inferring

Read each paragraph. Then read the sentences below it. If you can **infer** the correct ending for the sentence from the facts given in the paragraph, underline that ending. On the line below the sentence, copy the key word or words from the paragraph that led you to that inference.

If you **cannot** infer the answer from the facts in the paragraph, do not underline any of the sentence endings.

A. Janet slowly opened the door, got in, and sat down. Then she gradually pulled away from the curb. She waved good-bye and started out on her long journey.

1. Janet is getting into a (plane, house, car).

   door, got in, sat down, pulled away from curb

2. She is going (to the store, on a trip, to school).

   long journey

3. She will not return for several (weeks, days, months).

4. Her mood is (happy, nervous, solemn).

   slowly, gradually

B. The wind gently waved the new grass on the empty prairie. The sky was cloudless. The moon had just come up.

1. It is (morning, afternoon, evening). moon
2. The weather is (clear, threatening, cold). cloudless
3. The land is (flat, mountainous, forested). prairie

C. The fiery disc seemed white-hot overhead. The land was dry and barren. There seemed to be no hope of a rain cloud ever covering that fiery disc.

1. The disc is (the moon, a floodlight, the sun). fiery, white hot
2. The land is (mountainous, desert, woodland). dry, barren
3. There are (no, few, many) houses in the area.

Name ______________________

Teacher Note
Discuss with pupils their responses to the activities. Have them tell what facts in each selection led them to make certain inferences and why—in some situations—no inference could be made from the given facts.

Inferring

Read the following paragraphs from a story. Try to fill in information that you are not directly told about the characters in the story. Then answer the questions that follow.

Jana pushed hard with all her might. Tony could do nothing to help her but give words of encouragement. "One more push, and I think the wheel will come free. Just one more." Finally, one more hard push did it. The right wheel lifted out of the rut between the sidewalk and lawn with a jerk. Tony lurched forward, almost falling out.

"Phew! Sorry about that!" Jana panted.

"That's all right," Tony replied.

"We'll have to tell Dad about that sidewalk so he can fix it," Jana said.

The two proceeded up the walk. Thank goodness for the ramp that led past the front steps to the door of the house. Jana noticed the curtains were drawn. She wondered why, on such a nice, sunny day. After all, her father loved nice, sunshiny days.

Jana opened the front door, then got behind Tony to push him into the house. The darkness inside startled her. It took a few moments for her eyes to adjust. Then she thought she saw shapes rising up and moving toward her. Human shapes. Suddenly she heard a huge shout: "Surprise!"

Now put an **X** before each detail you could probably infer is true from reading the story.

X 1. Tony is in a wheelchair. ✓

____ 2. Tony was in a car accident.

X 3. Jana and Tony are brother and sister. ✓

____ 4. Jana is older than Tony.

____ 5. Jana and Tony live on a farm.

____ 6. It is summer.

X 7. People are throwing a surprise party. ✓

X 8. The curtains were drawn so that Jana could not see inside. ✓

____ 9. Tony knew about the party.

____ 10. Tony and Jana do not live with their mother. } NO mention of mother? Comma

Name ____

Teacher Note
Ask pupils to read from the story for evidence to support each inference they made.

SKILL 17

Changes in Word Meanings

We often understand the meaning of a word only when we hear or read it in **context**—that is, in connection with other words. This is true of even simple words, such as **trunk**. **Trunk** can mean **(1)** part of a tree, **(2)** part of an elephant, or **(3)** a large container in which to pack clothes or other belongings.

A. Above the word **trunk** in the sentence below, write the number of the meaning that applies to it.

3 2 1

The elephant picked up the trunk with his trunk and set it next to the trunk of the banyan tree.

B. Study each sentence and the underlined words in it. Then rewrite the sentence, replacing one of the underlined words with a word or phrase that has a similar meaning. You may use a dictionary.

1. He had the ill fortune of losing his fortune in the stock market.

   Answers will vary according to which underlined word the pupil decides to replace.

2. She was not the type to type for long hours at a time.

3. At the peak of his career, the explorer went to the peak of Mt. Everest.

4. He was last seen wrapped in a cape and walking along the shore of the cape.

5. She will study this at home in her study.

Name ____________________

Teacher Note
After pupils have completed the page, discuss the definitions of the underlined words in each sentence. Have pupils compare the sentences they have written, which will vary according to the underlined word they elected to change.

Changes in Word Meanings

A. A simple word—such as *run*—often can be combined with other words to form a phrase that has a special meaning. Read each sentence below and the expressions that follow it. Then, in the blank, write the expression that most sensibly fits the context of the sentence.

1. It is always pleasant to ___run into___ a friend.
   a. run over b. run out of c. run into

2. The detective ___saw through___ the man's alibi.
   a. saw through b. saw off c. saw out

3. Midway through the race, Leonard ___fell behind___.
   a. fell under b. fell behind c. fell off

4. The crowd ___looked on___ in amazement as the magician performed.
   a. looked out b. looked on c. looked over

5. In her appearance, Susan ___takes after___ her mother.
   a. takes after b. takes over c. takes to

B. In the first column below, copy the expressions you used in the sentences in part A. In the second column, write the meaning of that expression. You may use a dictionary.

Answers will vary. Possibilities:

	Expression	Meaning
1.	run into	meet
2.	saw through	understood the falsity of
3.	fell behind	failed to keep up
4.	looked on	watched
5.	takes after	resembles

Name ______________________

Teacher Note
Discuss the meanings of all the expressions given in part A, and have pupils explain why they made the choices they did. The expressions are *idioms*. Some pupils may enjoy looking for other idioms given in the dictionary after the entry for the words *run, saw, fell, look,* and *take*.

Changes in Word Meanings

As time goes by our language changes. Many words take on new meanings and often leave their old meanings behind. In the **Word Box** are ten such words. Read the **old meanings** and the **new meanings** below. Then choose the word from the **Word Box** that is being defined or described and write it on the line.

Word Box

person	duck	slip	left	snob
dice	girl	villain	tinker	gossip

		Old Meaning	New Meaning
1.	girl	a child of either sex	a young female
2.	villain	a farm worker	a wicked person
3.	left	weak, worthless	one side of something
4.	duck	to dive	to move one's head quickly
5.	slip	slime	to slide suddenly
6.	tinker	a mender of pans	to work in a useless way
7.	person	a character in a play	an individual
8.	snob	a shoemaker's helper	someone who snubs others
9.	dice	to give	to cut food in small bits
10.	gossip	a godparent	to chat idly

Name ______________________________

Teacher Note
After pupils have completed and checked their work, discuss their ideas about why word meanings may change through the years. Have pupils suggest slang terms currently in use in their own talk, and have them decide whether slang also changes through the passage of time.

Changes in Word Meanings

In Lewis Carroll's book *Through the Looking-Glass,* the main character—Alice—hears the following poem:

Twas brillig, and the slithy toves
Did gyre and gimble in the wabe:
All mimsy were the borogroves,
And the mome raths outgrabe.

Here is what Alice said about the poem: "It seems very pretty, but it's **rather** hard to understand! Somehow it seems to fill my head with ideas—only I don't know exactly what they are!"

A. Begin to unravel the mystery of the nonsense poem.
1. Draw **one** line under all the words you think are **nouns**.
2. Draw **two** lines under all the words you think are **adjectives**, or describing words.
3. **Circle** all the words you think are **action verbs**.

B. When you have completed part A correctly, you are ready to write your very own sensible version of the poem. Do this by filling in the blanks below with nouns, verbs, and adjectives of your own choosing. Poems will vary.

'Twas ________________, and the ________________ ________________
Did ________________ and ________________ in the ________________:
All ________________ were the ________________,
And the ________________ ________________ ________________.

C. Share your poem with your classmates. If the poem now makes sense, you have shown how well you know the English language and how skillfully you can work with it.

Name ________________

Teacher Note
After pupils have completed part A, ask them what clues they used to decide whether the nonsense words were nouns, adjectives, or verbs. (For example, the articles *a, an,* and *the* usually signal that a noun lies ahead.) After this discussion, some pupils may need to rethink their answers. Then have pupils complete parts B and C. (You might divide pupils into groups for part C.)

A. Ordering Objects Estimating

Labels and their placement will vary, but the total picture should show items organized in a logical way.

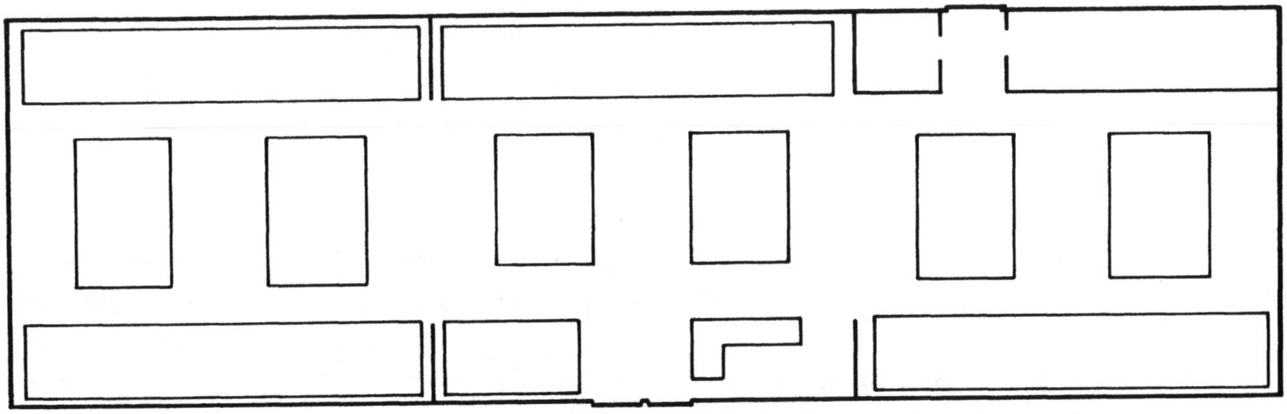

BACKDOOR

ENTRANCE

Mr. and Mrs. White have just bought a row of three stores. One is a stationery shop, one is a gift shop, and one is a hardware store. The Whites have combined the shops to make one large store which sells stationery, gifts, and hardware.

On the floor plan above, write labels to show how you would arrange and order the various items. Keep in mind that customers need to find the things they want easily and that the store must also look attractive and appealing.

Suppose that it is now October 1. The Whites have announced that the new store will open on October 12. On the lines list the tasks that must be carried out before the store can open.

Answers will vary. Possible responses are listed.

unpack goods

clean store

hire workers

arrange items on shelves

price items

B. Inferring

To buy and combine three stores is a big project. What inferences can you make about the Whites and the town they live in? Answers will vary. Possibilities:

The Whites have enough money to make a big investment.

The Whites are experienced storekeepers.

The town needs a large department store.

Name ____________________

Teacher Note
After completing the page, pupils may discuss and check their work with you or with a classmate.

C. Anticipating Probabilities

On opening day, Mr. White gave copies of the following memo to all the employees. Read the memo. Then, on the lines below it, tell two **probable** feelings or reactions the employees would have.

MEMO

To all employees:

It is imperative that all employees arrive at the store exactly one-half hour before its opening, which occurs at nine o'clock in the morning. Employees must be dressed suitably in freshly washed and pressed clothing. A list of official work assignments will be displayed on the framed bulletin board situated at the rear door of our establishment. Midday dining hours will be arranged for each employee after a conference concerning the necessity of keeping the store well-staffed throughout the shopping day. Employees may consider their duties completed at the evening hour of five o'clock, at which time they may return to their various homes.

1. Answers will vary. Possibilities: Employees will be confused. (or) Employees may be upset.
2. Employees may feel that the Whites will be hard to please.

D. Changes in Word Meanings

Mrs. White agreed with the rules in Mr. White's memo, but she felt that the memo was too wordy. She wants the memo rewritten so it is brief and clear. On the lines below, rewrite the memo in a way that would please Mrs. White.

Answers will vary but should be brief and complete.

Name

Teacher Note
After completing the page, pupils may discuss and check their work with you or with a classmate.

UNIT 4

Analyzing

Teacher Note

In order to develop Bloom's fourth stage—analyzing—the pupil needs to engage in the following skills:

- Judging Completeness
- Judging Relevance of Information
- Distinguishing Abstract from Concrete
- Judging Logic of Actions
- Organizing Elements of a Selection
- Examining Story Logic
- Recognizing Fallacies

Analyzing means seeing how parts fit together. Look at the picture. Why do you think the bird is sitting on the rhinoceros's back? Does the rhinoceros seem to care? How do you know? Can you assume this has happened before to the rhinoceros? Why or why not?

SKILL 18 Judging Completeness

When you prepare a report, you look for information that provides you with specific facts. Including important facts in your report helps make it complete.

Suppose that you are preparing a report on the Erie Canal. In three different sources, you find the three paragraphs below. Read the paragraphs. Then follow the instructions below them.

1. The Erie Canal was needed when it was built in the early 1800s. The canal went across the Mohawk Valley, which did not have many settlers. The canal was a success from the start.

2. Many settlers lived in eastern North America in the early 1800s. A canal was needed to help the people move West. A route was surveyed in 1810, and the canal was completed in 1825. It connected Lake Erie with the ocean. Traffic flourished until about 1900.

3. A canal trip was an exciting undertaking in the early days of our country. Migrating westward by way of the Erie Canal was a thrill unmatched. Many strange and beautiful sights unfolded before those who traveled aboard one of the Erie's horse-drawn barges.

A. Circle the paragraph that gives the most helpful information.

B. List the facts contained in the paragraph you chose. You should be able to list five facts if your listing is adequate and complete.

Answers should approximate those listed here.

1. In the early 1800s, many settlers lived in the East.
2. A canal could help people who wanted to move West.
3. A survey for a canal route was done in 1810.
4. The canal was completed in 1825, connecting Lake Erie with the ocean.
5. The canal was heavily traveled until about 1900.

Name ______________________

Teacher Note
After pupils have completed the page, discuss why the second paragraph would be the most helpful to a writer of a report. Have pupils compare the list of facts they wrote for part B and make any revisions they feel are needed.

Judging Completeness

When you are asked to perform a task, you need certain details in order to do the task correctly and efficiently. Imagine that you are in the following situations. Tell what you need to know before you can complete each task well. Answers will vary. Possibilities are given.

1. You work in a department store. A customer asks for a bicycle wheel. You need to know what kind of bicycle it is; the model number.

2. You work in a hardware store. A customer wants a new lawn mower and would like to have it delivered. You need to know what size lawn mower is wanted; how much the customer is willing to spend; where the customer lives.

3. Your school principal has asked your class to organize a school art show. Your class needs to know what grades will be participating; when the show will take place; what room or rooms will be used; who is to be invited to the show.

4. Your teacher has asked you to write a composition. You need to know the subject of the composition; how long it should be; when the composition is due.

5. Your parents have asked you to help organize a birthday party for a younger child. You need to know how old the child is; when the party will take place; where it will take place; how many guests there will be; what kind of food your parents want to have served.

Name ____________________

Teacher Note
After pupils have completed the page, discuss their responses. Have them tell why the things they listed are important if the task is to be completed efficiently.

Judging Completeness

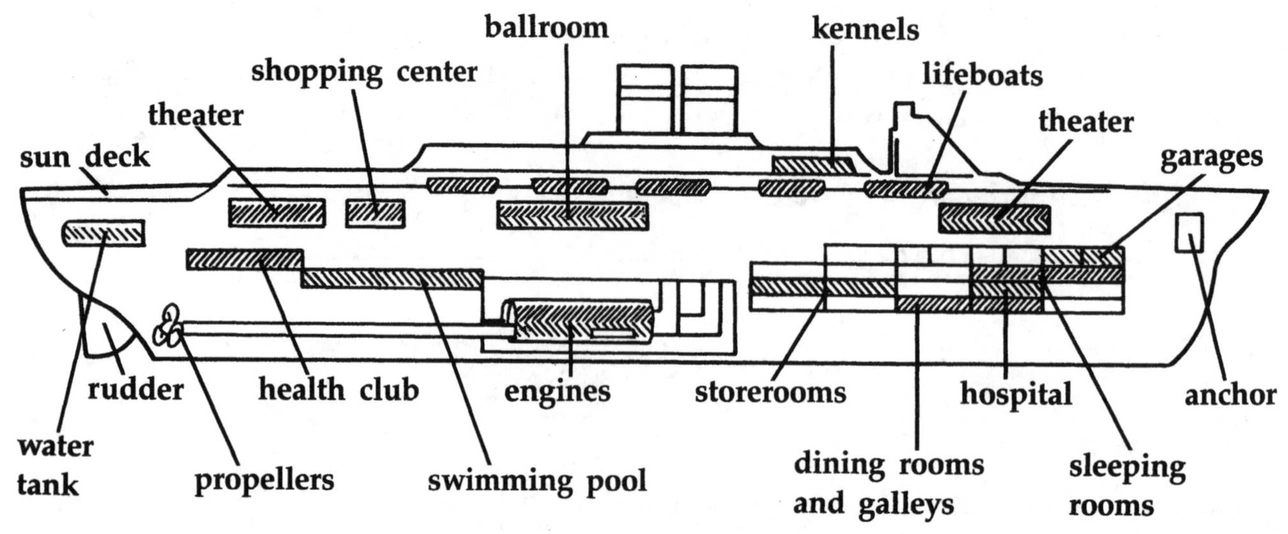

Cruise ships, or ocean liners, are huge seagoing hotels. There are often as many as a thousand workers, or crew, aboard to provide for the comfort, safety, and health of the passengers. Ocean liners can travel across the Atlantic over eight times before stopping for fuel, water, or supplies. Their galleys, or kitchens, can prepare meals which serve 9,000 daily.

Study the drawing of an ocean liner and read the paragraph. The sentences below refer to the drawing. Put **T** before each sentence which is true according to the drawing. Put **F** before each sentence which is not true according to the drawing.

__F__ 1. There is a place to get a haircut on the ship.

__F__ 2. The drawing shows where the fuel is stored.

__T__ 3. Two people could attend different movies at the same time.

__T__ 4. Passengers may transport their cars across the ocean on this ship.

__T__ 5. There are escape boats for the passengers in case of emergency.

__F__ 6. The swimming pool is on the sun deck.

__T__ 7. There is a special place for people who become ill.

__T__ 8. Passengers may bring their dogs on this voyage.

__F__ 9. There is a flight deck where planes can land on the ship.

Name ____

Teacher Note
After pupils have completed the page, have them point out on the ship diagram the visual information—or lack of it—that led them to make their responses. Discuss other kinds of visual devices that they expect to be complete (instructions for assembling a tool or other object, road maps, graphs and charts).

SKILL 19 — Relevance of Information

When information is **relevant**, it is important to the subject you are studying. **Relevant** information is to the point.

For each activity below, underline the **two** information sources that would provide you with the most relevant information.

1. You want to find a recipe for upside-down cake.
   recipe book   cookbook   magazine   newspaper
2. You want to know how to bandage a deep cut.
   magazine   science book   health book   first aid book
3. You would like to learn how to grow zinnias.
   gardening book   book on shrubs   book on soil
   instructions on a package of zinnia seeds
4. You need to know the names of the planets in our solar system.
   health book   astronomy book   astrology book   science book
5. You want to know how to spell and pronounce the word **pecuniary**.
   atlas   spelling book   dictionary   newspaper
6. You would like to become informed about different careers.
   social studies book   individual books describing careers
   newspaper articles   counseling books
7. You need to improve your handwriting.
   chart on cursive letters   spelling book   English book
   handwriting book
8. You are interested in the duties of nurses.
   hospital manual   health book   book about careers
   book of medical diseases
9. You are interested in the most recent scientific discoveries.
   science book   newspaper   encyclopedia   recent science magazines
10. You want to know how to install rear speakers in your car.
    book about engines   car owner's manual
    printed instructions that come with new speakers

Name ______________________________

Teacher Note
After pupils have completed the page, ask them to explain why the sources they selected would provide the most relevant information. Discuss the other sources listed; how some of them might provide relevant information but would not be a good first choice. For example, magazines and newspapers often have recipes. However, the likelihood of finding a recipe for upside-down cake would not be great.

Relevance of Information

Suppose that you are to write a report about life in the Amazon region of South America. From the 12 sentences below, choose the ten that you think are most relevant to the subject. Then organize the ten sentences into a paragraph, rewording where necessary.

1. Malaria is more common in tropical areas than in other places.
2. Mosquito netting is necessary equipment in this region.
3. Due to flooding and poor soil, the region does not have good farmland.
4. Large parts of the Amazon rain forest are disappearing.
5. The sun can cause serious sunburn even on a cloudy day.
6. Tropical rainfall is heavy and frequent.
7. Tropical rivers contain anacondas, alligators, and piranha.
8. The climate of equatorial regions is hot and humid all year.
9. Salt tablets may help to maintain body fluids in hot climates.
10. Boiling is one way to purify water for drinking.
11. A great variety of trees and plants grow in the Amazon region.
12. Here in this equatorial region the chief mode of travel is by boat along the Amazon River.

Paragraphs will vary but should contain the facts given in the ten relevant sentences above.

Sentences 9 and 10 are not relevant.

Name ______________________

Teacher Note
After pupils have completed the page, discuss why two of the listed sentences are comparatively irrelevant to the subject of the report. Pupils may wish to share their completed paragraphs by reading them aloud.

SKILL 20

Abstract or Concrete

Groups of words that name related objects can be ranked from **abstract** to **concrete**. Usually a word that names a **particular** person or object is most **concrete**. Words become more abstract as they name categories that include more and more objects or people.

A. In each sentence below, there are four words or word groups that are related. Study the sentence and underline these related words or word groups. Then write **1** over the word or word group that is most abstract. Use the numerals **2**, **3**, and **4** over the other words as you narrow them down to the most concrete. The first sentence has been done for you.

1. Mrs. Smith (4) was voted the best teacher (3) of all the personnel (2) working in our school system (1).

2. Henry Aaron (4) was one of the best home-run hitters (3) of all the batters (2) who have been major league baseball players (1).

3. Dogs (2) are among our favorite household pets (1), and the golden retriever (4) is perhaps the favorite kind of hunting dog (3).

4. Among the trees (2) chosen for yards, the maple (3) is one of the most popular, and the red maple (4) is one of the most spectacular of plants (1).

B. Rewrite each sentence below, replacing the underlined words with ones that are more concrete. Answers will vary.

1. He went into the room and prepared a meal. ______________________

____

2. She got into the vehicle and headed for the roadway. ______________________

____

3. We put the liquid into a container. ______________________

____

Name ____

Teacher Note
After pupils have completed part A, discuss the reasons for their choices and for their ordering them from *1* to *4*. Have pupils proceed with part B, and then discuss their responses, pointing out that the use of concrete words usually makes a statement more vivid and understandable to a reader or listener.

SKILL 20 Abstract or Concrete

Good writers usually try to use concrete words and phrases as much as possible. Such words and phrases help the reader see, understand, and analyze what the writer is telling about.

A. Read the following paragraph. Underline the concrete words and phrases that help you to see what the writer is telling about.

One summer evening while I was sitting on the verandah of our rambling old house in Riverdale, I saw a dark object sail downward through the dusk toward the base of a White Ash that stood about twenty feet away on the lawn. I heard a soft **plop** as the object landed. There was just enough light for me to see that it was a Flying Squirrel that had landed head-upward on the trunk of the tree just a few feet above the ground. Then it shot up the tree like a streak and disappeared.

—from *A Natural History of New York City* by John Kieran

B. Write a concrete word or word group from the paragraph above that can replace each abstract term in the list below.

1. a sound soft plop
2. a tree White Ash
3. a town Riverdale
4. a distance twenty feet few feet
5. an animal Flying Squirrel
6. a time of day evening (dusk)

C. Write a brief description of an animal—wild or domestic—that you have observed. Use as many concrete words and phrases as possible to make your description vivid to your readers. Answers will vary.

Ocelot

Name

Teacher Note
After pupils complete parts A and B, discuss their responses. Then have pupils proceed with part C and share the results with their classmates. Discuss with pupils the concrete words in their paragraphs that help to make their descriptions vivid to the reader.

Logic of Actions

Actions are **logical** if they **make sense** in helping you to achieve a specific goal.

A. Suppose that you are the oldest of three children. Your sister is six and your brother is four. Your parents have asked that the three of you do the following chores before they return home from work. Write **sister, brother,** or **myself** after each chore to show the logical person you would assign to each job. Answers will vary.

1. pick up toys ____________
2. rake leaves ____________
3. walk the dog ____________
4. feed the cat ____________
5. carry out the garbage ____________
6. take the grocery list and go to the store ____________
7. vacuum the living room rug ____________
8. renew some books from the library ____________
9. get the mail from the mailbox ____________
10. polish the children's shoes ____________

B. Suppose that it is holiday time. You have saved $16 with which to buy gifts for the following people: your parents, a younger brother or sister, a grandparent, your best friend. On the lines below, list in order at least five logical steps you would take before and during your shopping trip. Answers will vary.

1. ____________
2. ____________
3. ____________
4. ____________
5. ____________

Name ____________

Teacher Note
After pupils have completed the activities, discuss their responses. Encourage pupils to explain why they think their responses are logical and to determine why some of their answers may vary from those given by their classmates.

Logic of Actions

A. Parking places were difficult to find, even in 1926. In that year, someone invented a lightweight car which had a set of small wheels at the back. To park the car, a person stood it up on these wheels. Was this a logical solution to the parking problem? Answers will vary.

Why or why not? ______

______

Could we use this kind of solution to today's parking problems? Answers will vary.

Why or why not? ______

______

______

B. Two classes were planning a trip. They found three possible places to go. Their problem was that the classes could not choose which one they liked best. Finally, Rosa suggested that the teachers break the deadlock by choosing a different place from the three the students had suggested.

Was this a logical plan? Answers will vary.

Why or why not? ______

______

On the lines below, write a logical suggestion of your own to solve the classes' problem.

Answers will vary.

______

______

______

Name ______

Teacher Note
After pupils have completed the page, discuss their responses. Encourage pupils to accept responses that vary from their own, as long as the responses are logical. Stress that there are often several logical ways to solve a problem.

SKILL 22

Elements of a Selection

One important **element**, or **part**, of a story is the **setting**. The setting is **where** the story takes place. A good description of a setting can help you analyze why the story characters feel and act as they do. The description can also give you, the reader, a special feeling—such as comfort, fear, curiosity, or happiness.

The setting of the book *Charlotte's Web* is a farm. The paragraph below describes a very special part of that setting. Read the paragraph and write answers to the questions that follow it.

> The barn was very large. It was very old. It smelled of hay and it smelled of manure. It smelled of the perspiration of tired horses and the wonderful sweet breath of patient cows. It often had a sort of peaceful smell—as though nothing bad could happen ever again in the world. It smelled of grain and of harness dressing and of axle grease and of rubber boots and of new rope. And whenever the cat was given a fish-head to eat, the barn would smell of fish. But mostly it smelled of hay, for there was always hay in the great loft up overhead. And there was always hay being pitched down to the cows and the horses and the sheep.

1. Would you enjoy being in the place described above? Answers will vary.

   Explain why or why not? ______________________

   ____

   ____

2. Which word in the selection gives you the most important characteristic of the barn?

   smelled Why does the author use that word so frequently?

   This is the sense the author wishes to emphasize in the description.

   ____

3. Suppose the author had decided to use the sense of **hearing** as the basis for describing the setting of the barn. What details might such a paragraph include?

   Answers will vary but should allude to the various animals and things mentioned in the paragraph.

   ____

   ____

Name ______________________

Teacher Note
After pupils have completed the page, discuss their responses and encourage them to tell why answers to item 1 may vary. Pupils may enjoy constructing together a paragraph that includes some of the details they have listed independently for item 3.

Elements of a Selection

Read this selection from *The Adventures of Tom Sawyer.* Then answer the questions that follow.

Tom appeared on the sidewalk with a bucket of whitewash and a long-handled brush. He surveyed the fence, and all gladness left him and a deep melancholy settled down upon his spirit. Thirty yards of board fence nine feet high. Life to him seemed hollow . . . .

He took up his brush and went tranquilly to work. Ben Rogers hove in sight presently—the very boy, of all boys, whose ridicule he had been dreading . . . .

"Hello, old chap, you got to work, hey?"

Tom wheeled suddenly and said: "Why, it's you, Ben! I warn't noticing."

"*Say*—*I*'m going in a-swimming, *I* am. Don't you wish you could? But of course you'd druther *work*—wouldn't you? Course you would!"

Tom contemplated the boy a bit, and said: "What do you call work?"

"Why, ain't *that* work?"

Tom resumed his whitewashing, and answered carelessly: "Well, maybe it is, and maybe it ain't. All I know is, it suits Tom Sawyer."

"Oh come, now, you don't mean to let on that you *like* it?"

The brush continued to move.

"Like it? Well, I don't see why I oughtn't to like it. Does a boy get a chance to whitewash a fence every day?"

That put the thing in a new light. Ben stopped nibbling his apple . . . . Presently he said: "Say, Tom, let *me* whitewash a little."

1. What kind of boy do you think each character is? Answers will vary.

   Tom is clever. Ben makes fun of others and is easily fooled.

2. What do you think will happen next in the plot?

   Tom will get Ben to whitewash the fence.

3. Why do you think the author had the boys say words like *ain't* and *druther?*

   He wanted them to sound like boys from a particular area in the United States.

   He also wanted to show that the conversation taking place was informal.

Name ____________________

Teacher Note
Ask pupils to support their answers with evidence from the selection.

Story Logic

A story is **logical** if it is told in an order that makes sense. Usually this order relates to time. The author begins with what happened first and ends with what happened last.

A. The outline below is not written in the correct time sequence. Rewrite the outline on the blank lines so that the sequence is correct.

Charles Dodgson	**Charles Dodgson**
II. Later life	I. Early life
A. Wrote *Alice in Wonderland*	A. Born in 1832
B. Died in 1898	B. Teacher of mathematics
C. Took the pen name Lewis Carroll	II. Later life
I. Early life	A. Took the pen name Lewis Carroll
A. Teacher of mathematics	B. Wrote *Alice in Wonderland*
B. Born in 1832	C. Died in 1898

B. Use your rewritten outline to write a short paragraph about the life of Charles Dodgson. Keep the facts in the correct sequence.

Paragraphs will vary but should be sequential.

Name ______________________

Teacher Note
After pupils have completed part A, discuss their rewritten outlines with them. Then have them proceed with part B. Have pupils share their paragraphs by reading them aloud. Instruct listeners to check to make sure that the paragraph follows time sequence and includes all the main ideas and details given in the rewritten outline.

Story Logic

Seven sentence parts are listed in the box. Decide where each sentence part fits logically within the article, and write it in the blank.

1. act as cleanup squads for debris	5. three body segments
2. two pairs of wings	6. outer skeletons
3. three-fourths of all animal life	7. provide food
4. climate and food supply	

An insect is an animal with an outside skeleton, a shell-like covering, and usually two pairs of wings. An adult insect has six legs, and its appendages have joints. Insects have three body segments These are the head, thorax, and abdomen.

Our world is teeming with insects. Insects comprise about three-fourths of all animal life on our planet. Though most insects are tiny and live less than a year, they have not become extinct for several reasons. They have adapted to changes in climate and food supply; they are able to reproduce quickly; their bodies are protected by outer skeletons; and they are able to escape danger by flying.

While many kinds of insects are harmful, other kinds are useful. Insects provide food for birds, fish, and other small animals. Insects also pollinate plants and act as cleanup squads for debris

DRAGONFLY

TERMITE

BUTTERFLY

Name ______________________________

Teacher Note
After pupils have completed the page, have one pupil read his or her completed paragraph, while other pupils check responses against their own. Pupils may wish to revise their paragraphs if they have inserted sentence parts in illogical positions.

SKILL 24 Recognizing Fallacies

A **fallacy** is an error in reasoning. Be on the lookout for fallacies in **either-or** statements. An **either-or** statement says that only two choices are possible. Sometimes this is true. For example, **You are either in school or not in school**. Often, however, there are other choices possible besides the two in an either-or statement.

Each statement below is an **either-or** fallacy. Change each one so that it is **not** a fallacy. The first one is done for you. Answers will vary.

1. People have either dogs or cats for pets. ____________________

   People may have dogs, cats, birds, hamsters, and many other kinds of animals as pets.

2. Either it is raining or the sun is shining. ____________________

   ____

   ____

3. A person is either your friend or your enemy. ____________________

   ____

   ____

4. Water is contained in either lakes or bays. ____________________

   ____

   ____

5. Fish may be eaten either with butter or with lemon. ____________________

   ____

   ____

6. Either you play with a group or you don't play at all. ____________________

   ____

   ____

Name ____________________

Teacher Note
After pupils have completed the page, discuss their rewritten statements. Encourage pupils to revise any responses that appear, on the basis of the discussion, to be fallacious.

Another kind of fallacy is the **slanted argument**. In a slanted argument, the writer or speaker presents information in a way that is meant to convince you to think or act in a certain way. Here are some methods used in slanted arguments:

1. **Use of glad words:** words that make you feel positive and enthusiastic about a person or a product.

2. **Bandwagon technique:** statements that try to make you feel that "everyone else" is doing something, so you should, too.

3. **Famous-person endorsement:** statements that well-known public figures support an idea or use a product.

A. Read each slanted argument below. Then write the number of the slanted argument method that is being used.

1. All across the nation, it's the Lemon-Aid generation! 2
2. Rock star Emmy Emerald eats Raisin Cane Cereal every day! 3
3. This soft, velvety cream makes skin feel silky smooth. 1
4. Vote Row A on Election Day to get fair play and honesty in government. 1
5. Smart families rely on Safety Swoop Sirens. How about your family? 2

B. For each sentence below, choose and write the phrase that would probably make the best slanted argument out of the sentence.

1. ask for — insist on — are interested in

People in-the-know insist on Mo-Go Motor Oil.

2. many Americans — hungry people — actor Lance Lotmore

Bit-o-Burger is the quick meal preferred by actor Lance Lotmore.

3. adventure-filled — very nice — safe and quiet

To drive the Galaxy 2000 is to have a new, adventure-filled experience.

Name ______________________

Teacher Note
After pupils have completed part A, discuss where they are most likely to hear or read such "slanted arguments" (radio, television, advertising in magazines and newspapers, billboards). After part B is completed, ask pupils to explain why they made their choices.

Recognizing Fallacies

A true **analogy** is a statement which shows the relationship between two pairs of words. The first pair of words shows what the relationship is about. Here are some examples:

- **Up** is to **down** as **over** is to **under**. (Relationship: opposites)
- **Second** is to **minute** as **hour** is to **day**. (Relationship: part of)
- **Clock** is to **time** as **scale** is to **weight**. (Relationship: function)

A. Write **opposite, part of,** or **function** after each analogy.

1. **Ounce** is to **pound** as **inch** is to **foot**. part of
2. **Saw** is to **cut** as **shovel** is to **dig**. function
3. **In** is to **out** as **beautiful** is to **ugly**. opposite

B. Make each analogy true by choosing the correct word to complete it.

1. **Rug** is to **floor** as **blanket** is to bed.
   warm bed wool
2. **Needle** is to **sew** as **hammer** is to hit.
   metal tool hit
3. **Shy** is to **bold** as **quiet** is to loud.
   loud silent sleep

C. The analogies below are false, because the last word in each one is incorrect. That is, the last word does not continue to show the relationship set up in the first pair of words. Cross out the last word. On the line, write the word that will make the analogy true.

1. **Scissors** are to **cut** as **rulers** are to ~~**color**~~. measure
2. **Foot** is to **leg** as **hand** is to ~~**body**~~. arm
3. **Happy** is to **sad** as **fast** is to ~~**quick**~~. slow
4. **Pencil** is to **writing** as **brush** is to ~~**comb**~~. painting
5. **Car** is to **drive** as **airplane** is to ~~**wing**~~. fly

Name ______________________

Teacher Note
After pupils have completed parts A and B, discuss their responses and help them correct any errors. Then have pupils proceed with part C. Discuss their responses and have them explain the relationship in each analogy.

SKILL 24 Recognizing Fallacies

An **assumption** is an idea we reach before we have all the facts. Some assumptions turn out to be true. Others, however, turn out to be false. When all the facts are gathered, the assumption may prove to be wrong.

Read each item below. On line **1** make an assumption about the situation. On line **2** write why the assumption may be wrong. Answers will vary.

A. A man climbs up a fire-escape and opens a window to an apartment.

1. ______________________________

2. ______________________________

B. Amy plays the tuba. She decides to try out for the school band. On the day of the tryouts, Amy sees a long line of students waiting by the band room. Amy goes home.

1. ______________________________

2. ______________________________

C. Don grabbed the lunch bag and hurried to the cafeteria. As he began eating, Clark came over. "That's my lunch," said Clark. "My name is written on the bottom of the bag." Clark turned the bag over. There was the name **Clark**.

1. ______________________________

2. ______________________________

D. Sara was not doing well at school. She daydreamed in class. She seldom completed her homework. She was not willing to participate in class activities. When called on, her answers were usually wrong.

1. ______________________________

2. ______________________________

Name ______________________________

Teacher Note
After pupils have completed the page, discuss their responses. Have them compare their assumptions and the reasons they gave to show that the assumptions may be wrong. Discuss the two items that are examples of a special kind of assumption called "guilt-by-association" (items *A* and *C*).

A. Elements of a Selection

Read the poem. Then do the activities that follow it.

The Bird of Night

A shadow is floating through the moonlight.
Its wings don't make a sound.
Its claws are long, its beak is bright.
Its eyes try all the corners of the night.

It calls and calls: all the air swells and heaves
And washes up and down like water.
The ear that listens to the owl believes
In death. The bat beneath the eaves,

The mouse beside the stone are still as death —
The owl's air washes them like water.
The owl goes back and forth inside the night,
And the night holds its breath. —Randall Jarrell

1. What is the **setting** described in the poem? night in the woods
2. Name the main character in the poem. an owl
3. Is the main character real or fanciful? real

B. Judging Completeness

List three phrases from the poem that help make the description of the owl complete.

1. Answers will vary.
2. ______
3. ______

C. Logic of Actions

Why is it **logical** that the bat and the mouse stay very still as the owl flies by?

They do not want the owl to catch them.

Name ______

Teacher Note
After completing the page, pupils may discuss and check their work with you or with a classmate.

D. Recognizing Fallacies
Story Logic
Abstract or Concrete
Relevance of Information

Read the person's words. Then follow the directions that tell you how to rewrite the person's statement. Answers will vary. Possibilities:

1. Rewrite the statement so that it is not an **either-or** fallacy.

   You probably will like some kinds of birds better than other kinds.

2. Rewrite the statement so that it tells logically what the children are watching.

   I think birds are fascinating.

3. Rewrite the statement so that the words **These birds** are replaced by more concrete words.

   Ostriches and penguins can't fly.

4. Rewrite the statement so that it tells where to find relevant information about myna birds.

   If you read a book about pet birds, you can find out how to teach a myna bird to talk.

Name ______________________

Teacher Note
After completing the page, pupils may discuss and check their work with you or with a classmate.

UNIT 5

Synthesizing

Teacher Note
In order to develop Bloom's fifth stage—synthesizing—the pupil needs to engage in the following skills:
- Communicating Ideas
- Planning Projects
- Building Hypotheses
- Drawing Conclusions
- Proposing Alternatives

Synthesizing means putting information together to come up with new ideas. Look at the picture. What is the boy doing? How do you think the boy learned the dance? Have you ever added new ideas to a traditional song or dance? What was it like?

Communicating Ideas

A **concept** is a general idea we have about an object or a process. For example, the concept we have about **written information** is that it will be presented to us in fully spelled-out words and complete sentences. Sometimes, however, written information is presented in an **abbreviated** form. In such cases, you have to adjust your thinking so that you can understand the message.

In the following classified advertisements from a newspaper, the information is abbreviated. Study each advertisement. Then rewrite it in sentence form with the words fully spelled out. Answers will vary slightly. Possibilities:

1.

FURNITURE SALE—Auto washer, 2 dr refrig, b & w TV, 4 pc BR set, 5 pc din set, misc lamps. E–Z terms.

We are having a furniture sale. We are selling an automatic washer, a two-door refrigerator, a black-and-white TV set, a four-piece bedroom set, a five-piece dining room set, and miscellaneous lamps. We can offer you easy terms for payment.

2.

NEED EXEC SECY—typ 70 wpm, shthnd, fil. Local ofc of nat'l co. Paid hosp ins, 2 wk vac, top hrly pay. 40 hr wk. Apply 8–5, M–F.

I need an executive secretary who can type 70 words per minute, take shorthand, and file. The job is in the local office of a national company. The employee will get paid hospital insurance, a two-week vacation, and top hourly pay for a 40-hour week. Apply 8 a.m. to 5 p.m., Monday through Friday.

Name ____________________

Teacher Note
After pupils have shared their fully written-out advertisements, discuss with them the reason for using abbreviations in a classified ad. (Ad space is sold by the line, and buyers of that space attempt to get as much information as possible into a minimal number of lines.)

Communicating Ideas

A map can give you a fast visual idea of how water and land are related in space. Below is a map of the state of South Dakota, which is located in the northern part of the United States. Study the map. Notice where smaller rivers join to form larger rivers with new names.

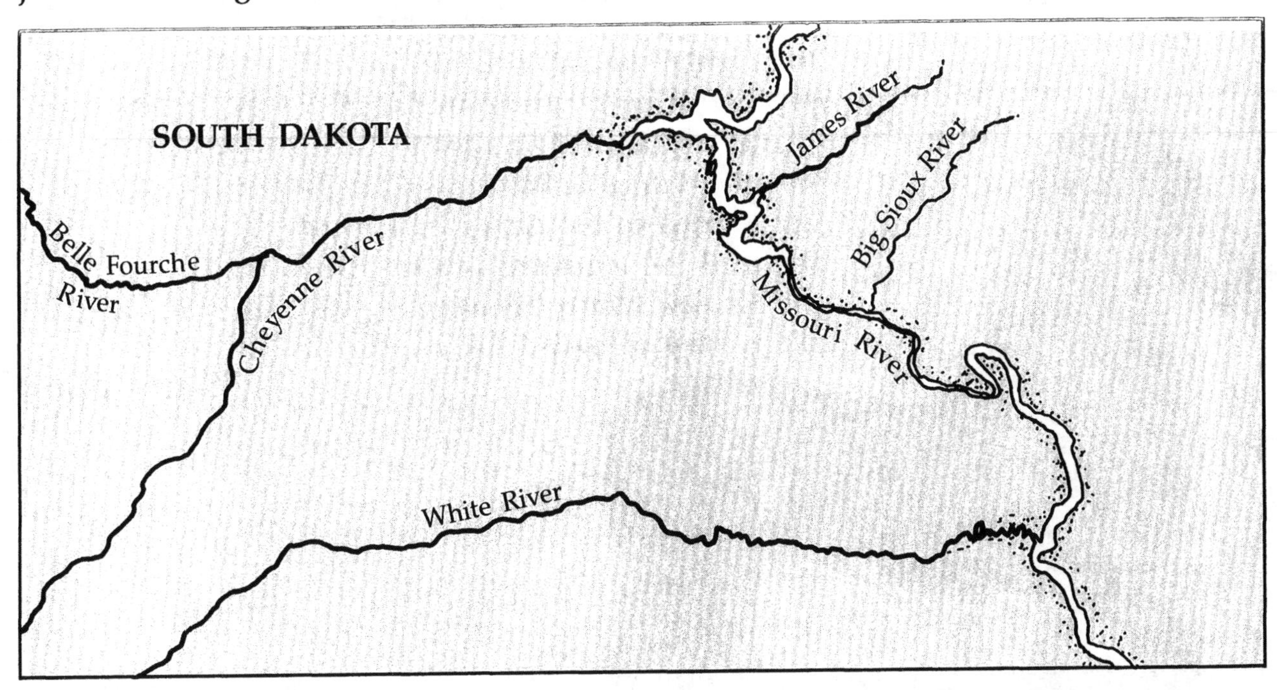

A. On the lines below, write a paragraph that describes the river system shown in the map.

Answers will vary.

B. Which type of communication—the map or the paragraph—makes it easier to understand the river system? Probable answer: the map

Tell why you think so. Answers will vary but most will state that some concepts are easier to understand in visual form than in verbal form.

Name __________

Teacher Note
After pupils have shared their work, discuss other visual information forms they have studied—in this book and elsewhere (graphs, charts, diagrams, pictures, photographs, codes, and so on).

Communicating Ideas

Artists and writers present the same idea in different ways. Study the statue of a horse. Then read the selection from a poem which tells about a special kind of horse, the Morgan. Write answers to the questions which follow the picture and the poem.

The Runaway

Once, when the snow of the year was beginning to fall,
We stopped by a mountain pasture to say, "Whose colt?"
A little Morgan had one forefoot on the wall,
The other curled at his breast. He dipped his head
And snorted to us. And then he had to bolt.
We heard the miniature thunder where he fled
And we saw him or thought we saw him dim and gray,
Like a shadow against the curtain of falling flakes.

—Robert Frost

1. What does the statue tell about a horse that the poem does **not** tell you?

Answers will vary.

2. What does the **poem** about a horse tell you that the statue **cannot** tell you?

Answers will vary.

Name ______________________

Teacher Note

After pupils have shared their work, discuss images that people have when the word *horse* is mentioned. Have pupils tell about the picture they see in their "mind's eye" when you say *horse*. Then discuss the ways in which all these images are alike, that is, the ways in which the concept *horse* is a shared one.

Planning Projects

Suppose you are assigned a book report. You can make your report in any form you like.
Answers will vary.

1. You decide to write your book report. Place the number **1** before each item you would probably need to make your report.

______	book	______	notebook paper
______	scissors	______	cassette tape player
______	other people	______	stiff cardboard
______	roll of paper	______	markers or paints
______	pen or pencil	______	box
______	tape (mural)	______	encyclopedia
______	costumes	______	props

2. Suppose you decide to make a mural showing what happened in the story you read. Place the number **2** before each item you would probably need to make your report.

3. Now suppose you decide to present a skit showing a scene from the story you read. Place the number **3** before each item you would probably need to perform a skit.

4. You must plan ahead so that you will have enough time to do your report. Which kind of report would probably take the most time to make? the skit

5. What must you do regardless of the kind of report you make?

   choose and read a book

6. Describe the type of book report you would prefer to do.

   ______

   ______

Name ______

Teacher Note
Discuss with pupils how to allocate time when planning a project. Often, a person must "work backwards," that is, estimate how long each step takes, add the times together, then work back from the end date to determine when he or she must start the project.

Planning Projects

Suppose that your class has been asked to plan a talent show for all the pupils in Grades 1 through 6. In the show, there must be several performers from each classroom. The principal has asked that the show be approximately one-and-a-half hours long.

You have one month to prepare for the show. On the lines below, list specific jobs that must be assigned to people in your class, such as **talent scout** and **director**. Briefly tell what the person holding that job must do. Answers will vary. Examples:

1. Talent scout—go to classrooms to ask for and audition performers

2. Director— coordinate the work of actors and other performers

3. Stagehands—move sets, take care of lighting, curtains

4. Scenery designer—design sets, find people to paint and build them

5. Publicity Person—make sure the show is advertised and announced properly so that a big audience will attend

Name ______________________

Teacher Note
After pupils have shared their work, discuss the ways in which the people holding the different jobs must work together if the project is to be completed successfully. Discuss differences of opinion that might arise between a talent scout and a director, or between a stagehand and a scenery designer. Have pupils consider how such differences of opinion might be resolved.

Planning Projects

On Earth Day, members of the Science Club decided to clean the park across the street from their school. Below is an outline of their plan. Read each step to find out if their plan is complete. Add another idea to each step. Answers will vary.

1. **Things to Do Before:**

Get permission from principal.
Get permission from park district.

Other: Scout park to determine how much litter there is; find out where to put garbage bags.

2. **Materials Needed:**

Recyclable plastic bags to collect garbage

Other: ties to close bags; gloves to pick up messy garbage

3. **Steps to Follow:**

Divide park into sections and assign groups of students to each section.
Each group moves through its section, collecting garbage.

Other: assign pupils to collect bags as they are filled and to distribute more garbage bags

4. **Time Needed:**

Time to divide into groups = 5 minutes

Time to pick up garbage = depends on amount of garbage and size of park—advance scouting required

Other: time to get to and from the park

Name ____________________

Teacher Note
Discuss pupils' answers. You may want to divide the class into small groups and assign each group an area of planning to evaluate.

Planning Projects

A. Think about the following projects. Underline the one that you would prefer to carry out.

1. Show the effect of temperature and light on the growth of bean seeds.
2. Make a floor plan and model of the ideal school.
3. Identify ten birds common to your area by making drawings and recording the different birdcalls.

B. Complete the following lists to show how you would begin the project you selected in part A. Answers will vary according to the project chosen by the pupil.

Supplies Needed

1. ____________________ 4. ____________________

2. ____________________ 5. ____________________

3. ____________________ 6. ____________________

Five Major Steps to Take

1. ____
2. ____
3. ____
4. ____
5. ____

People to Consult or Ask for Help

1. ____
2. ____

Name ____

Teacher Note
After pupils have shared their work, discuss changes they might like to make in their responses, based on what they learned from their classmates. Stress that the planning of a project usually requires adjustments and corrections before the project gets underway.

Building Hypotheses

A **hypothesis** is a beginning explanation of what is happening or why something happened. A hypothesis may change as new facts are gathered.

The true story below is given in three parts. Read each part and answer the question that follows it. Then continue reading the story.

1. In the summer of 1890, millionaire Harry Lehr invited his friends to a dinner party. His friends were excited because he told them that a very special guest would be there. Mr. Lehr's wealthy friends were used to important people, but they were curious about the identity of this special guest.

   Who do you think the guest might be?

   Answers will vary. Example: It might be a famous actor or political figure.

2. As the special guest entered the room, the other guests gasped in surprise. It was the Prince del Drago! He was attired elegantly in a black suit and tie. During dinner, however, the Prince did not talk to anyone. Silently, he ate his dinner.

   Why do you think this special guest was silent?

   He might be shy or he might not speak English.

3. When he finished eating, the Prince left the table and jumped to the huge chandelier. Then he unscrewed the light bulbs and threw them crashing down onto the table.

   Circle the picture below that identifies the Prince del Drago. On the lines below the pictures, tell what facts in the story led you to this hypothesis.

Answers will vary. Examples: He could not talk. He caused other guests to gasp. He could jump onto the chandelier. He played a monkey-like trick.

Name ______________________

Teacher Note
Before pupils undertake the activities, point out that *hypothesis* is the singular form of *hypotheses*. When pupils have completed and shared their responses, discuss the reasons why additional facts may cause one to make changes in a hypothesis.

Building Hypotheses

A. Five hypotheses and ten statements are listed below. Each hypothesis can be supported by facts. Which statements provide the facts that support each hypothesis? Write the letter of each statement before the hypothesis it supports. You will use more than one statement to support each hypothesis.

Hypotheses

e, h 1. Insecticides are not necessarily a sure way to kill mosquitoes.

a, f 2. The bathtub is one of the most dangerous areas in the home.

b, i 3. Some people dislike poetry.

c, j 4. Typewritten papers usually receive higher grades than handwritten papers.

d, g 5. Driver-training courses contribute to highway safety.

Statements

a. The hard material can cause broken bones and severe bruises.

b. Often it was not a part of their early learning.

c. They are easier to read.

d. Participants learn traffic laws and defensive driving attitudes.

e. There is proof that areas frequently sprayed still have many insects.

f. The enamel surface is so slippery that one can fall easily.

g. Driver-training graduates have fewer accidents than untrained drivers.

h. Some mosquitoes fly out of range of the spray.

i. Perhaps the subject was not presented in an interesting manner.

j. They have a more professional look.

B. Choose one of the hypotheses above. Write another statement to support it.

Answers will vary.

Name ______

Teacher Note
After pupils have shared their work and corrected any errors, discuss the difference between a *hypothesis* and a *guess*: a hypothesis is based on some facts already at hand; a guess is based on clues not yet formulated as facts.

SKILL 27 Building Hypotheses

Read the selection below. Then answer the questions that follow it.

Frédéric Chopin, the Polish composer, was visiting a friend in France—a woman named George Sand. As Chopin and Sand talked, they watched in delight as Sand's little dog raced around the room, chasing its tail, rolling on its back, and pursuing imaginary cats and mice. The puppy became exhausted and flopped to rest for a few seconds. Then it got up and began its wild games again.

Chopin laughed. He walked to the piano. Quickly he put together a composition which seemed to whirl and circle. Midway in the composition, Chopin put in a quiet part in which the music seemed to rest. Then the music picked up speed again. This piano composition—put together in such a happy spirit and with very little pre-planning—became one of Chopin's most famous piano pieces. It is known as "The Minute Waltz."

1. What inspired Chopin to write "The Minute Waltz"?

   Answers will vary. Examples: He watched a little dog romping around.

2. What facts in the story led you to make the hypothesis you stated in item 1?

   Chopin laughed at the dog. The musician went immediately to compose a piece which was as fast as the puppy's actions.

3. In what ways does "The Minute Waltz" reflect the movements of the little dog?

   It is fast, then slows briefly, then picks up speed again.

4. Musicians get their ideas from many sources. On the basis of the facts in the story above, what hypothesis can you make about one of these sources?

   One source is the rhythm involved in everyday actions.

Name ______________________________

Teacher Note
After pupils have shared their work, discuss other hypotheses they might make about the source of musicians' ideas. Encourage pupils to refer to their favorite musical groups and to discuss the ways in which these groups borrow ideas from one another.

Building Hypotheses

A. Three situations are described below. Write two hypotheses to explain each situation. Answers will vary. Possibilities are given.

1. A circus truck stops at a baseball field.

   a. A circus will be set up on the field.

   b. The driver of the truck is lost.

2. A stranger gets into your teacher's car and drives away.

   a. The stranger is stealing the car.

   b. The stranger is a garage mechanic who has agreed to pick the car up.

B. 1. Choose one of the hypotheses you wrote for part A and copy it below.

   Answers will vary.

2. Now list three facts you would need in order to show that your hypothesis is a valid, or true, one.

   a. Answers will vary.

   b.

   c.

Name

Teacher Note
After pupils have shared their work, discuss the difference between a *hypothesis* and a *theory*. A *hypothesis* is a *beginning* explanation, based on *some* facts. A *theory* is an explanation based on a large body of facts and tested evidence and has a higher degree of probability than a hypothesis does. Ask pupils why we refer to the *theory* of gravity, rather than to a *hypothesis* of gravity.

Drawing Conclusions

A **conclusion** is a final statement you can make based on the facts given to you. Read the articles below. Make a check by each conclusion that could **not** be made from the facts given in the article.

A. Soil may be described as the earth's cover where the land stops and the air begins. Every ounce of fertile soil normally contains more living organisms than the human population of the entire world.

The soil provides a very effective sewage and waste disposal system. Earth's materials are recycled in the soil as life goes through generation after generation. It is unfortunate that much soil has been damaged through misuse, erosion, and the use of harmful chemicals.

__√__ 1. Even poor soil is full of living things.

______ 2. Good soil contributes to the cycle of life on Earth.

__√__ 3. The earth's surface is covered with soil.

__√__ 4. People have deliberately damaged the soil.

__√__ 5. Scientists have carefully studied soil.

B. On May 25, 1961, U.S. President John Kennedy announced that the U.S. would land a person on the moon before the end of the decade. This tremendous mission cost $24 billion. The goal was finally reached when Apollo 11 landed on the moon's surface on July 20, 1969. Neil Armstrong, Edwin Aldrin, and Michael Collins were on board Apollo 11. Armstrong and Aldrin spent twenty-one hours and thirty-seven minutes on the moon before returning to the command ship.

__√__ 1. Three astronauts walked on the moon.

______ 2. The Apollo trip was costly.

______ 3. President Kennedy was interested in the trip to the moon.

__√__ 4. Several people wanted to go on the moon mission.

__√__ 5. The astronauts faced incredible dangers.

Name ____________________

Teacher Note
As pupils discuss their work, ask them to point out not only why each *checked* statement does *not* follow from the information given, but also *where* in the article they find facts that make each *unchecked* statement a valid conclusion.

Drawing Conclusions

You can reach conclusions by carefully studying a picture or a scene. Each conclusion below can be reached by putting together various details shown in the illustration. Write the facts that lead to each conclusion. Probable responses:

1. There are five people in the family.

   The table is set for five people.

2. One family member is about three or four years old.

   There are a tricycle and teddy bear in the yard—toys a toddler would use.

3. Someone in the family uses a wheelchair.

   There is a ramp next to the steps.

4. The family has at least two pets.

   There are a doghouse and a large cage.

5. It is springtime.

   Leaves are on the trees. It is warm enough to eat outdoors. People have been doing springtime gardening.

Name

Teacher Note
After pupils have discussed their completed work, ask them to suggest other conclusions they might reach by studying the picture—for example, conclusions regarding the location of the home, the care the family gives to the home, the size of the dog the family owns (based on the size of the doghouse), what other pet might be kept in the cage (a rabbit) and what chore was being done, as indicated by the shovel and hoe.

Drawing Conclusions

If you understand someone's personality, you can often conclude what he or she will do in a certain situation. The pupils described below must take part in a class play. Read about each pupil. Then tell what particular task the pupil is likely to volunteer to do in the play.

1. Dirk is extremely shy. He is, however, interested in watching plays, movies, and television dramas. It is not the actors that interest Dirk so much as it is the lighting and sound effects used in the productions.

2. Carla seems to have a special gift for working with color. Her friends always admire her paintings. She dresses in an original way. She has a knack for combining her clothes so that she always looks very special.

3. Mario is a great talker. He likes to tell jokes and is always ready to give colorful descriptions of things that have happened to him. Even from a distance, you can always identify Mario's voice, which rings with laughter.

4. Francine has a collection of notebooks in which she is always writing. One notebook is a journal about her personal experiences. Another notebook contains Francine's story ideas. In still another notebook, Francine lists interesting words she finds as she reads or as she listens to people talk.

5. When pupils are arguing over what game to play or what project to carry out, they very often call on Marta to settle the dispute. She has a way of solving problems and organizing activities that makes her classmates like and respect her.

Probable responses:

Dirk's job in the play:

He will plan the scenery, lighting, and sound effects.

Carla's job in the play:

She will design the costumes.

Mario's job in the play:

He will be an actor or announcer.

Francine's job in the play:

She will help write the play.

Marta's job in the play:

She will be the director.

Name ______________________

Teacher Note
After pupils have shared their work and made any revisions that seem necessary, discuss the tasks the individuals described on this page might undertake in another sort of project, such as putting on a science fair.

Drawing Conclusions

In the script of a play, the dialogue and the directions (in parentheses) help you draw conclusions about the characters. Read the following part of a script. Then answer the questions.

Ariel ***(shaking slightly)***: I do not want to cross this foggy swamp! At night it is filled with goblins and other dreadful creatures. ***(She pulls away from Cassie.)***

Cassie ***(extending her hand to Ariel)***: Oh, come along, Ariel! Don't be such a fearful thing. There is magic that will protect us. And besides, we must cross the swamp and rescue the Prince before the sun rises.

Ariel ***(moving toward Cassie again)***: Oh, yes. The Prince! We can't break our promise to him. But what is the magic, Cassie? What do you mean when you say **magic**?

Cassie ***(smiling)***: If you will come with me, Ariel, you will see that the magic is inside you. The name of the magic begins with the letter **C**. Now do come along!

Ariel ***(taking Cassie's hand)***: The letter **C**. . .what could that be? **Calm**? **Curiosity**? **Caring**? Oh, this is all too scary and puzzling for me! ***(Ariel and Cassie move into the foggy swamp as the howl of the Swamp Goblin fills the air.)***

1. What kind of person is Ariel? Answers will vary. Possibilities: She is timid. She trusts Cassie. She wants to keep her promise.

2. What kind of person is Cassie? Answers will vary. Possibilities: She is brave. She, too, wants to keep her promise. She tries to give courage to others.

3. Does this play tell a story of fantasy or a story of reality? Fantasy.

   How do you know? It has goblins and a haunted swamp in it.

4. Imagine that Ariel and Cassie are now in the middle of the swamp. Write another line of dialogue for each character.

   Answers will vary. Dialogue, however, should suit the personalities of the characters as shown in the script and as described in 1 and 2.

Name ______

Teacher Note
As pupils share their responses, ask them to identify the clues that led them to the conclusions. Discuss how they decided to write particular lines of dialogue in response to item 4.

Drawing Conclusions

One day Samantha announced to her friends that she was a math wizard. "To prove this," said Samantha, "I want each of you to follow these steps:

1. Write a three-digit number in which the first and last digit differ by at least 2.
2. Reverse the digits in your number and write the new number.
3. You should now have two three-digit numbers. Subtract the smaller number from the larger one. Write down your answer.
4. Reverse the digits in your answer and write the new number.
5. Add this new number to your answer in step 3."

After Samatha's friends finished, Samantha whispered to each of them, "Your final answer is 1089." In each case, Samantha was absolutely right!

A. What is your conclusion about Samantha's magic trick?

The answer to this process is always 1089.

B. On the lines below, test your conclusion by following steps 1 through 5 as given above.

C. Check your conclusion again by asking a classmate or your teacher to carry out the steps.

D. Suppose your classmate or teacher comes up with an answer that is not 1089. What will your conclusion be?

The classmate or teacher has made a mistake in carrying out one of the steps.

Name ______________________

Teacher Note
After pupils have completed and shared their responses, discuss why it is often necessary to test a conclusion by gathering more evidence. (The conclusion may not be correct.)

Drawing Conclusions

Read the following passage from a book. Then answer the questions. Answers will vary. Possibilities are given.

Fire!

In that instant Murchison pressed the button of the ignition device, thereby establishing the current and hurling an electric spark into the depths of the cannon. A terrible, thunderlike detonation ensued, the likes of which had never been heard before, with such roaring and flashing that it exceeded anything imaginable. A huge column of fire shot out from the ground as from a crater. The earth trembled; some of the spectators momentarily caught sight of the projectile, as it triumphantly shot through fiery vapors up into the atmosphere. The streak of white-hot flame which rose to the heavens spread its light over all of Florida. . .

from *Journey from the Earth to the Moon* by Jules Verne

1. The author of the passage was making a living as a poet, playwright, and accountant. He had, however, become bored in the company of poets, actors, and bankers. So he began to visit the library frequently, studying another subject which interested him. What do you conclude that the subject was?

   Science or technology because the details in the passage show a knowledge of rockets.

2. The passage was written by Jules Verne and comes from his book *Journey from the Earth to the Moon*. The book was published in 1863. Some of Verne's other books are *Twenty Thousand Leagues Under the Sea*, *Journey to the Center of the Earth*, and *The Mysterious Island*. What kind of books do you conclude that these are?

   They are science-fiction books.

3. Jules Verne became known as "the man who invented the future." From this nickname, what do you conclude about the things Verne told about in his books?

   He told about machines, processes, and adventures that did not take place in his lifetime but soon would, in our century.

Name ______________________

Teacher Note
After pupils have completed and shared their responses, discuss the way in which they synthesized given information to come up with valid conclusions. Help pupils to see that in *synthesizing*, they are actually putting facts together to come up with an idea of their own.

SKILL 29

Proposing Alternatives

There is usually more than one way to solve a problem. When you offer another solution, you are **proposing an alternative**. Read each item below. Then propose an alternative to the solution given. Answers will vary. Possibilities are provided.

1. Your teacher tells you to measure a distance in meters but you can find only a yardstick. You decide that measuring the distance in yards is better than not measuring it at all.

   Use the yardstick. Then use the formula for converting yards to meters.

2. You lost a button on your shirt. To keep your shirt closed, you fastened it with a safety pin. Now the pin is making a tear in your shirt.

   Remove the pin. Hold the shirt together with a piece of two-sided tape.

3. Your class is giving a play. Five students have volunteered for the leading role. One student says he should be given the part because he did well in the last class play.

   Have each of the five students try out for the part. Then the other students, the teacher, or the director can decide who gets it.

4. Your class has a new word game. The game is played with two teams. Ten players are needed on each team. Since there are twenty-two students in your class, you tell two of your classmates that they will have to be left out of the game.

   One student can be the scorekeeper and the other can keep track of the time, check players' answers.

5. You have worked hard to prepare your oral book report. Today is the big day! All of a sudden you discover that you left your notes at home. You decide to give your report without your notes even though you know that it won't be very good.

   Call a parent and ask him or her to bring your notes or ask your teacher if you can give your report tomorrow.

Name ______________________

Teacher Note
After pupils have completed their work, have them share their responses. Discuss the value of brainstorming as a method of finding alternative solutions to a problem. Help pupils recall recent occasions in the classroom when they have actually done this sort of brainstorming to solve a real-life problem.

Proposing Alternatives

Write at least one alternative item you could use or one action you could take in each situation. If you can't think of an answer, you can **brainstorm.** To brainstorm, write down as many ideas as you can think of, without stopping to judge whether each idea makes sense. Once you are through brainstorming, go over your answers and cross out those that probably would not work. Answers will vary.

1. If you can't find scissors, what else could you use or do to cut a piece of paper straight?

ruler, straight edge, fold then tear paper

2. If you can't find a circle compass, what else could you use to draw a perfect circle?

any object having a round edge

3. If you can't find a watering can, what else could you use to water plants in a small pot?

water pitcher, any container used with a funnel

4. If you can't find a paper clip, what else could you use or do to hold papers together?

staple, rubber band, fold over upper left corners

5. If you can't find a shoelace, what else could you use to tie your shoe?

string, ribbon, yarn

6. If you can't find your raincoat, what else could you use or do to keep from getting wet?

umbrella; a large, plastic bag; hold a newspaper over head

Name ____________________

Teacher Note
Ask pupils to explain their answers. Discuss the idea of brainstorming—how it can be a useful technique as long as one later evaluates the list of responses.

Proposing Alternatives

Study the following story and the picture that illustrates it. Then write three sentences which propose alternatives **you** might take if you actually found yourself in this situation.

One Saturday morning, as Mark walked along a seldom used path in the park, he found an expensive wrist watch on the shore of the lake. As Mark examined the watch, a man approached him.

"Give me that watch!" demanded the man. "I saw you pick it up. That watch belongs to me. Hand it over right now!"

Alternatives: Answers will vary. Possibilities:

1. Give the watch to the man immediately.

2. Ask the man to identify the watch, then either give it to him or tell him that the watch is not his at all.

3. Explain the situation to the police officer.

Name ____________________

Teacher Note
As pupils compare their responses, discuss some of the considerations that should be taken into account in a situation such as the one described: physical safety, real effectiveness of a course of action, and whose role it actually is to determine the ownership of the watch.

SKILL 29 Proposing Alternatives

Study the situation described below. As you read, imagine that **you** are the baby-sitter.

> One night, Leon accepted a job as baby-sitter for his neighbors' child, Chrissy. The first part of the evening went well. Leon fed Chrissy her supper, read her a story, and tucked her into bed. After Chrissy fell asleep, Leon went downstairs to the kitchen and started to do his homework.
>
> Suddenly, there was a howl from Chrissy's bedroom. Leon rushed upstairs. Chrissy was holding her stomach in pain. Tears were running down her cheeks. Leon felt Chrissy's forehead. It was as hot as a firecracker!
>
> "Hold on, Chrissy!" said Leon. He ran downstairs again to look at the telephone message pad. Chrissy's parents had forgotten to leave important information! There was no doctor's number, no number that told where Chrissy's parents could be reached, and no numbers of neighbors or friends to call.
>
> Chrissy was sick and needed help. Leon knew that!

What are three alternatives Leon could take in this situation? Answers will vary. Possibilities:

1. Call his parents.
2. Find the number of his own doctor, and ask that doctor for help.
3. Run next door and ask a neighbor to help him.

Name ______________________________

Teacher Note
After pupils have compared their responses, discuss situations in which they themselves have had to rapidly consider alternatives for handling an emergency situation.

Proposing Alternatives

Hula hoops were once extremely popular toys. The picture shows you how they were used. Although the hula game is out-of-date now, there might still be ways to use the leftover hoops.

A. Describe how you could use a hula hoop in each case below.

Answers will vary.

1. To teach someone how to tell time

____

____

2. For use in a relay race, where people run from one point to another

____

____

3. To show social studies data, such as population groups within a certain area

____

____

4. To teach someone about fractions ______________________________

____

5. For use in an art project ______________________________

____

B. On the lines below, describe another use for leftover hula hoops.

____

____

Name ____

Teacher Note

After pupils have completed the page, discuss their responses and have them suggest ways in which other "abandoned toys," such as yo-yos, could be used.

Proposing Alternatives

In the book *The Middle Moffat*, the author—Eleanor Estes—tells about Janey Moffat, the middle child in a large family. Janey has many projects. One of them is to help her neighbor, Mr. Buckle, live to be one hundred years old. Mr. Buckle is already ninety-nine years old. To help him reach his one hundredth birthday, here are some of the things that Janey Moffat does:

- She follows Mr. Buckle from a distance as he leaves the library to make sure no dogs jump on him and scare him.
- As Mr. Buckle passes the firehouse, Janey reminds him of how loud the fire siren can be, so that he will not be startled by the noise.
- Janey follows Mr. Buckle with an umbrella, just in case it may rain. She does not want him to catch cold.
- Janey does not want Mr. Buckle to trip and hurt himself. She clears the path from the library to Mr. Buckle's home by kicking aside such things as fallen branches, orange peels, and broken glass.

Suppose that you are Janey Moffat. Propose some other things you could do to help Mr. Buckle reach his one hundredth birthday.

Answers will vary.

Name

Teacher Note
After pupils have completed the page and compared their responses, discuss the ideas and values Janey Moffat probably has that lead her to care for Mr. Buckle. Pupils can also discuss other actions they have observed or taken out of concern and affection for another human being. Help pupils to see that we synthesize our values and beliefs into ways of acting.

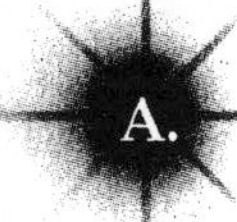

A. Communicating Ideas
Drawing Conclusions
Proposing Alternatives

Study the material in the boxes. Then do the activities.

Message from a Caterpillar

Don't shake this
bough.
Don't try
to wake me
now

In this cocoon
I've work to
do.
Inside this silk
I'm changing
things

I'm worm-like now
but in this
dark
I'm growing
wings.

—Lilian Moore

Four Stages in the Life of a Butterfly

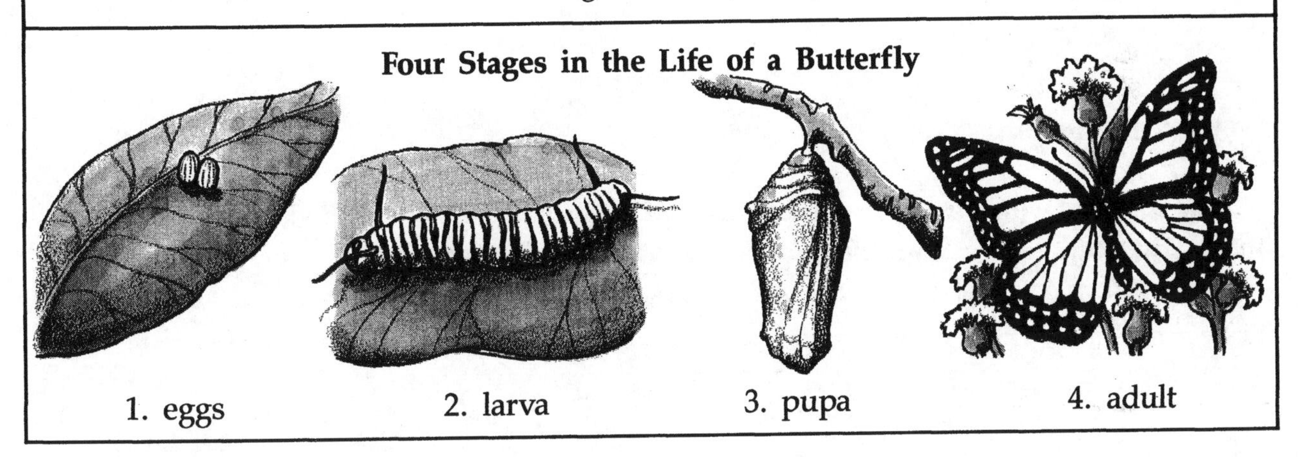

1. eggs 2. larva 3. pupa 4. adult

1. The materials above present the concept of **change**. In what two forms is the concept presented? The concept is presented in poetry form and in picture form.
2. From the information given in the boxes, what insect stage do you conclude that the poet is telling about? pupa

   What key words and phrases support your conclusions?

   Answers will vary. Examples: bough, cocoon, inside, I'm changing, worm-like now, growing wings
3. Propose an alternate way of telling about insect change. Answers will vary.

Name ______________________

Teacher Note
After completing the page, pupils may discuss and check their work with you or with a classmate.

B. Building Hypotheses

The pictures at the bottom of the page show four of the many kinds of animals that migrate.

1. Write a hypothesis telling what may cause some animals to migrate.

   Answers will vary.

2. Name some of the sources you would consult to find out whether your hypothesis is correct.

   Answers will vary.

C. Planning Projects

Imagine that you have been asked to join an oceanographic expedition to study the migration path of the humpback whale. Describe what specific job you would like to do in this project. Tell about the materials and skills you would need.

Answers will vary.

caribou

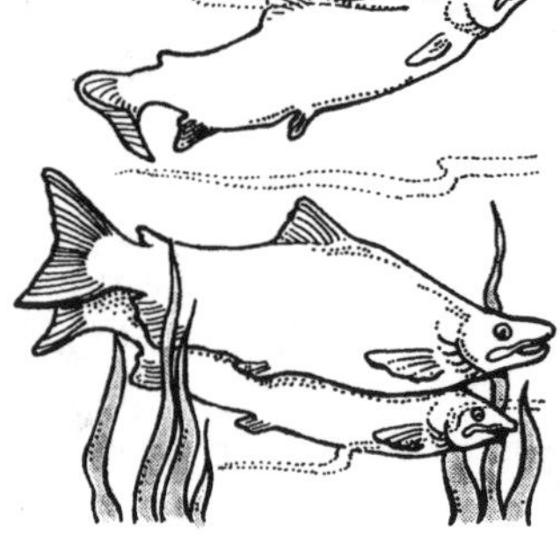

salmon

geese whales

Name

Teacher Note
After completing the page, pupils may discuss and check their work with you or with a classmate.

UNIT 6

Evaluating

Teacher Note

In order to develop Bloom's sixth stage—evaluating—the pupil needs to engage in the following skills:

- Testing Generalizations
- Developing Criteria
- Judging Accuracy
- Making Decisions
- Identifying Values
- Interpreting the Mood of a Story

Evaluating means making a judgment or decision about something. Look at the picture. What are the athletes doing? Why should all athletes stretch their legs before participating in a sport? What are some other things athletes can do to get ready for an event?

Testing Generalizations

Aesop's fables are stories that lead to generalizations about people's behavior— even though the characters in the fables are most often animals. Read each fable and choose the generalization from the box that fits the fable. Then explain whether the generalization is always true or whether in some real-life cases it is not. Answers will vary.

Generalizations
The rich get richer, and the poor get poorer.
Greed will only make you lose what you already have.
Little by little does the trick.

A crow was half-dead from thirst when it came upon a pitcher. Hopefully, it put its beak into the pitcher, but found only a little water left in the bottom. It tried and tried, yet it could not reach the water. Then a thought occurred to the crow. It took a pebble and dropped it into the pitcher. Then the crow took and dropped another pebble, and another, and another. Eventually, the water rose high enough, and the crow was able to drink.

Little by little does the trick; not always true

A dog was trotting home with a fine, meaty bone it had found, when it came upon a plank bridge crossing a stream. As the dog walked across the plank, it looked down and saw its reflection in the water. But the dog thought it was seeing another dog—one with an even larger and meatier bone. It made up its mind to have that bone, too. So it opened its mouth to snap the bone away from the other dog, dropping its own bone into the water and losing it forever.

Greed will only make you lose what you already have; not always true

Name ____________________

Teacher Note
Ask pupils to explain why they think each generalization is or is not always true.

Testing Generalizations

Each generalization below states something that is not always true. Write a sentence of your own to show that the generalization is false, or **invalid**. Answers will vary but should include qualifying phrases.

Example: Atomic energy is dangerous.
Atomic energy has been put to use to cure diseases.

1. Students who go out for athletics are not interested in schoolwork.

2. Exposure to sunlight causes skin cancer.

3. People who use surfboards like the feeling of danger.

4. Everyone should have a telephone-answering machine.

5. People who run for a political office only want power.

6. If you eat junk food, you are bound to get sick.

7. Television shows give you false ideas about the world.

Name ______________________

Teacher Note
After pupils have shared their responses, discuss where they are apt to run across invalid generalizations (advertisements, commercials, political-campaign speeches, and so on). Pupils will also benefit from discussing why invalid generalizations can be dangerous to people who do not take time to analyze them.

Testing Generalizations

Read each paragraph. On the lines below it, write a true, or **valid**, generalization you can make from the facts given in the paragraph. Answers will vary.

1. Imagine what would happen if all the glass around you should suddenly disappear! Insulated glass is used for windows, because it lets in light but keeps out hot and cold air. Glass is used in light bulbs, television tubes, mirrors, camera lenses, and eyeglasses. Even some cooking utensils and curtains are made of glass.

___

___

___

2. Have you ever examined the rings in a tree stump? Each ring is the result of one year's growth. Therefore, counting the number of rings will tell you the approximate age of the tree. The width of the rings shows whether the tree grew a lot or just slightly during a year. If the tree was damaged or diseased during its growth, that might result in fuzzy or partial rings.

___

___

___

3. Much of the land around the equator in Africa is densely forested wilderness. Tall trees spread their branches, shading the ground with heavy foliage. Near the ground, vines and creepers climb the trees and hang from limb to limb. The shady ground is covered with a thick growth of bushes with stems and branches so closely connected that it is difficult to clear a path without cutting the growth with each step.

___

___

___

Name ___

Teacher Note
After pupils have completed the page and compared their responses, discuss the ways in which a valid generalization is like a main-idea, or topic, sentence. Help pupils realize that a *valid* generalization is helpful in that it briefly and accurately summarizes a collection of related facts.

Developing Criteria

A **criterion** is a rule or guideline for judging or evaluating something. (The plural form of **criterion** is **criteria**.)

1. Suppose that your criterion for a tool is that it must measure time. Study the pictures below. Make an **X** on the tool or tools that do not meet that criterion.

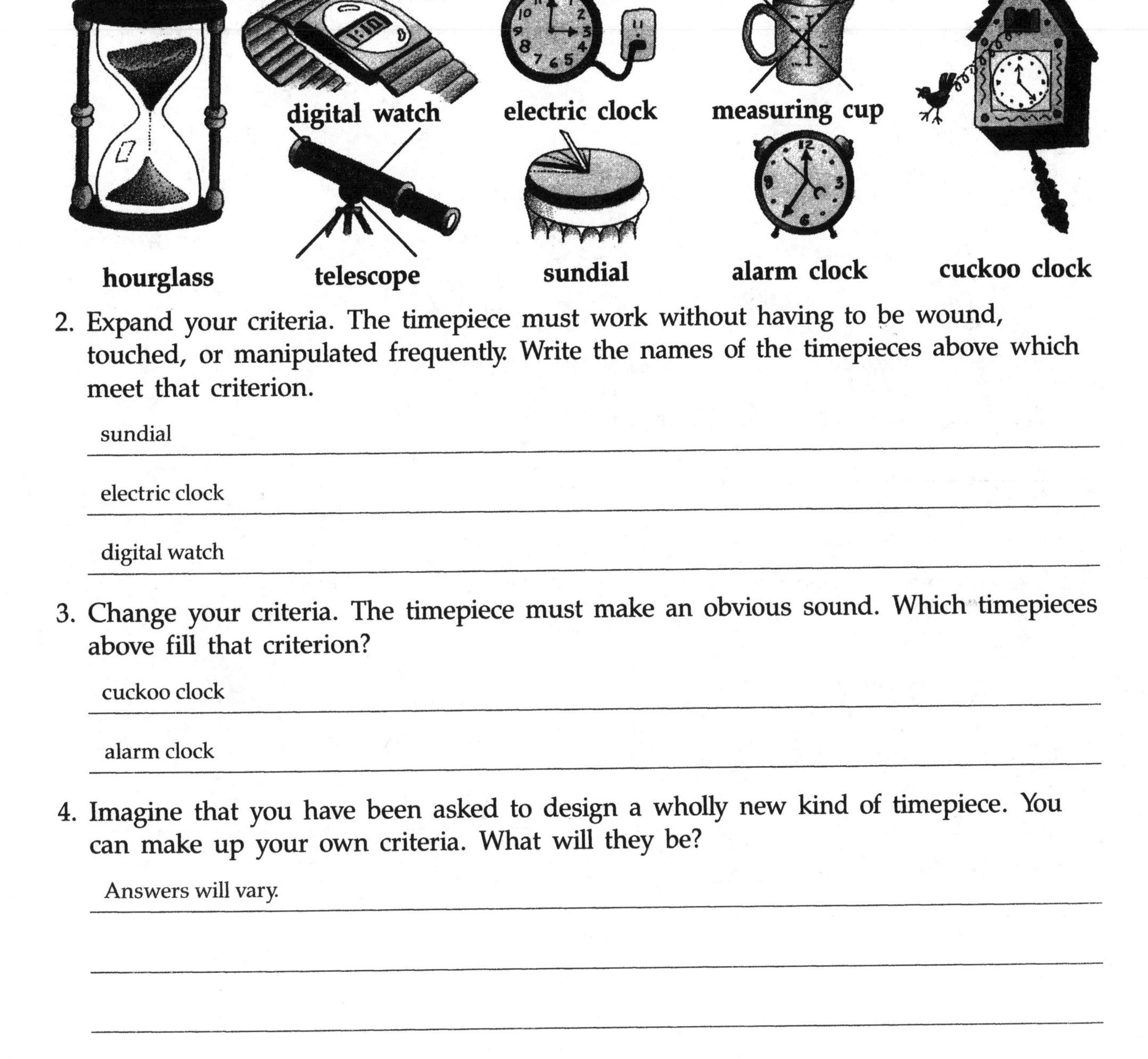

2. Expand your criteria. The timepiece must work without having to be wound, touched, or manipulated frequently. Write the names of the timepieces above which meet that criterion.

sundial

electric clock

digital watch

3. Change your criteria. The timepiece must make an obvious sound. Which timepieces above fill that criterion?

cuckoo clock

alarm clock

4. Imagine that you have been asked to design a wholly new kind of timepiece. You can make up your own criteria. What will they be?

Answers will vary.

Name ______________________

Teacher Note
After pupils have completed the page and shared their responses, discuss the different sets of criteria they follow each day, such as criteria for behavior at home and at school, criteria for submitting reports, compositions, and other homework assignments, and criteria involved in playing different sports and games. Encourage pupils to brainstorm about what would happen if there were no criteria for any of these situations.

Developing Criteria

As you read, you often come across words that are unfamiliar to you. As a criterion for figuring out a word's meaning, you can use the context—or sentence—in which the word is used. As new details are provided in the sentence, your idea about the word's meaning can change.

Read sentence **1**. Use only the information in sentence 1 to fill in the blanks in the sentence below it. Next read sentence **2**. Use the information provided in sentence 2 to fill in the sentence below it. Continue in this manner for all the sentences on this page.

scarf
mosaic glass
wooden block

1. Betsy was given a **tessera**.

   A **tessera** could be a scarf, a mosaic glass, or a wooden block.

2. Betsy was given a **tessera** that had a hard surface.

   A **tessera** could be a mosaic glass or a wooden block.

3. The **tessera** had a hard surface that reflected light.

   A **tessera** is a mosaic glass.

lion
garment
bird

4. Did you see the **ouzel**?

   An **ouzel** could be a lion, a garment, or a bird.

5. Did you see the **ouzel** eating its meal?

   An **ouzel** could be a lion or a bird.

6. Did you see the **ouzel** eating seeds and berries?

   An **ouzel** is a bird.

Name ______________________

Teacher Note
Have pupils complete the page and check their work. Then ask them to think of a criterion writers could follow when they use unusual or unfamiliar words in their writing. (They could put these words in a context that allows readers to determine its meaning.)

Developing Criteria

Suppose that your class is having a Riddle-Search Contest. You must find riddles that follow different criteria.

Criterion 1: Find a riddle that **does not** rhyme.

Criterion 2: Find a riddle that **does** rhyme.

1. Write **Criterion 1** or **Criterion 2** above each riddle below.

Criterion 2

A box without hinges, key, or lid,
Yet golden treasure inside is hid.

— from *The Hobbit* by J.R.R. Tolkien

Criterion 1

I can go up the chimney down,
But not down the chimney up.

2. On the lines below, write your own riddle to follow Criterion 1.

Answers will vary.

3. Now write your own riddle that follows Criterion 2.

Answers will vary.

4. Develop your own criteria for the Riddle-Search Contest. For example, you might specify that all riddles must be on a certain subject, or that all riddles must be based on homophones (words that sound alike). Write your Riddle-Contest criteria below.

Answers will vary.

Name

Teacher Note
After pupils have completed and shared their work, discuss with them the criteria we expect authors of different kinds of work to follow, for example, writers of biography, writers of science textbooks, writers of poetry, writers of science fiction.

SKILL 31 Developing Criteria

Writers often follow certain criteria as they compose stories and poems. Here are the criteria for the poetry form called **haiku**:

- A **haiku** has three lines.
- When spoken aloud, the first and third lines have five syllables.
- When spoken aloud, the second line has seven syllables.

A. Does the following poem meet the criteria for a haiku? To find out, make a mark over each syllable in the poem.

> An old silent pond . . .
> A frog jumps into the pond,
> splash! Silence again.
> —*Basho*

B. Complete the following sentence by first circling the correct word or word group in parentheses and then finishing the sentence in your own words.

The poem by Basho (**is, is not**) a haiku, because it has three lines, with five syllables in the first and third lines, and seven syllables in the second line.

C. Another kind of poem is called a **tanka**. Here are the criteria:

- A **tanka** has five lines.
- The first and third lines have five syllables each.
- The second, fourth, and fifth lines have seven syllables each.
- A **tanka**, like a **haiku**, usually tells about a scene from nature.

On the lines below, write your own tanka. Keep the criteria in mind.

Answers will vary.

Name ____________________

Teacher Note
After pupils have completed the activities and shared and checked their poems, discuss the challenge involved in following a strict set of criteria. Encourage pupils to tell about the different problems they encountered in adhering to the criteria for a *tanka* and how they solved these problems.

Judging Accuracy

When you read or listen, evaluate the accuracy of what the writer or speaker is saying. For example, listen or read to make sure there are no **contradictions**. In a contradiction, a person says one thing, and then later on says something that is just the opposite.

Read the following selections. Find and underline the sentences in each that contradict one another.

1. You can learn a lot by raising a young animal that you have found in the wild, such as a red squirrel or a raccoon. If you find a wild animal that is hurt or sick, call your local Humane Society. The people there will urge you to return the animal to its natural environment. When you raise a wild pet in your home, the Humane Society will gladly help you out.

2. In every state in the United States, it is a law that children must attend school until a certain age. Unless you attend school until that age, you or your parents could be taken to court. The law allows that "school" can mean being taught at home by your parents or going to a private school. In Mississippi, there is no law about attending school.

3. Most Americans respect George Washington, our first President, and have a special regard for his honesty. When Washington was only six years old, he admitted to his father that he had cut down a prized cherry tree. There is little doubt that Washington valued honesty and loyalty in government. The story about the cherry tree was made up by a man named Parson Weems, who sold 50,000 copies of his book about George Washington's life.

4. Children who run away from home often feel that they have very good reasons for doing so. Home may be a place where there is a lot of trouble and fighting, and it's best to stay away. Home is still the place where you can get the best help. Runaway children can get back home by calling one of the many "hotlines" for runaways.

Name ______________________________

Teacher Note
After pupils have shared and compared their responses and made any necessary corrections, discuss what they have learned from the activity that they can put to use when they are revising their own written or oral reports.

Judging Accuracy

When you are reading or listening, check to make sure that the conclusion follows logically from the facts that are given. If the conclusion does that, then it is accurate.

Study the picture and words below. Then do the activities.

A. What is the speaker's conclusion? He concludes that people should vote for him.

B. Why are the two young people in the audience doubtful about the conclusion?

There are no facts to support it.

C. Imagine that you are the speaker's speech writer. List three possible facts that the speaker could use to justify the conclusion "Vote for me!"

1. Answers will vary but should deal with the speaker's background and experience.

2. ______

3. ______

Name ______

Teacher Note
After pupils have completed the page, discuss again the implication of the page so far as the preparation of their own reports goes: *Conclusions should be supported by facts.*

Judging Accuracy

Good writers provide their audiences with specific and vivid details. Their words, phrases, and sentences give evidence that they have studied their subjects well and have thought about them thoroughly.

Read the following paragraphs. As you read, think about the statements the author is making. Do they seem exact and accurate?

> Swim out over a coral reef, and you see coral shaped like rocks, stars, fingers, or fans. There is coral shaped like animal horns and antlers, even like trees and bushes. There is coral of all colors—tan, orange, yellow, purple, green, and pink.
>
> A coral reef is an underwater range of stone hills. It forms in the shallow, warm oceans of the world. The warm temperature of the water and a good supply of sunlight are needed for the coral to grow. It is built up, bit by bit, over thousands of years by the remains of sea plants and animals. The largest coral reef in the world is the Great Barrier Reef off the coast of Australia. It is hundreds of feet wide and over one thousand miles long.
>
> — from *The Coral Reef* by Gilda Berger

Now answer these questions about the selection.

1. Which paragraph makes you think the author might have seen a coral reef herself?

   the first paragraph

2. Does each sentence seem accurate to you? Are there any facts that seem hard to believe?

   Answers will vary.

3. Which would be the best way to check the information in this selection?

   ______ ask your teacher

   __x__ look in an encyclopedia

   ______ go scuba diving near a reef

Name ____________________

Teacher Note
After pupils have completed the page, discuss with them situations when one is willing to accept the author's word and situations when one might feel the need to check another source. Also discuss the kinds of sources that are good references.

Judging Accuracy

Sometimes, when you are reading or listening, you come upon a statement that makes you say to yourself, "That doesn't sound right! That doesn't fit in with what I already know."

Follow through with your feelings. You may be wrong, or you may be right. Maybe you have found some evidence that the writer or speaker was in error. Do some research and find out for sure.

Read the items below. Circle the ones that seem to have one or more obvious errors in them. Check the facts. Then rewrite the items you have circled to make them accurate.

1. Teenage girls are involved in more automobile accidents than are teenage boys.
2. The era of clipper ships was not one for cowardly sailors. The workers who handled these steamships were known for their courage and daring.
3. A **dowel** is a peg which is used to fasten two pieces of wood together.
4. Your science project will go well if you simply act on your own and ignore the advice of other people.
5. Most Spanish place names in North America can be found in the northeastern part of the continent.

Answers will vary.

Name ______

Teacher Note
After pupils have completed the page and compared their responses, discuss the term *common sense* and how it can be used to evaluate a speaker's or writer's words. Encourage pupils to see that they already have a great deal of information about the world and are developing the thinking skills that can help them assess other people's pronouncements.

Making Decisions

On many occasions, you are expected to provide **evidence** to prove that what you are saying is correct. Read about each situation described below. On the lines, write the kind of evidence you would expect each speaker to present.

Answers will vary, but all should focus on the necessity to present facts and evidence.

1. One evening, a police officer stopped a driver who was moving along through traffic without using headlights. "I'm sorry, Officer," said the driver. "My headlights don't work. I just called the garage and was going there now to get the lights repaired."

2. The historical committee in a town asks that construction of a new housing project be stopped. "The site of the project," said the committee chief, "is an ancient Indian burial ground. It contains many valuable artifacts and should be preserved as a special forever-wild area."

3. The manufacturer of a new kind of glass claims that the product should be used for windows. A spokesperson for the company said, "The glass is unbreakable, conserves energy by keeping warm air from escaping, and lets in more light than other kinds of glass."

4. You announce after lunch that you found a valuable ring on the playground. "Hey, that's my ring," says one of your classmates. "I'm glad you found it. Please give it to me."

Name

Teacher Note
After pupils have completed the page, discuss the kinds of evidence they established as necessary in each instance.

SKILL 33 Making Decisions

In preparing a report, you are usually expected to use resource material to find facts about your subject and to check those facts. Read each subject below. Then look at the book titles in the picture at the bottom of the page. Write the titles of the books that you could consult for evidence.

1. a report on local moths and butterflies

   Encyclopedia, Vol. 8, M-N; *The Encyclopedia of Natural History; Field Guide to Insects*

2. a report on the rain forests of New Guinea

   Rand-McNally World Atlas; Travels in the South Pacific (also possible: *The Encyclopedia of Natural History)*

3. a report on nursing as a career

   Encyclopedia, Vol. 8, M-N; *Careers for You*

4. a report on English words from other languages

   Webster's College Dictionary; Words and Their Meanings

5. a report on the development of the highway system

   The History of Transportation

Name ______

Teacher Note
After pupils have completed the page and shared their answers, discuss the outside sources they themselves have used in preparing reports. Have pupils determine why many books of nonfiction have bibliographies at the end of them.

Making Decisions

The best decisions are made when you develop criteria for testing your decision. For example, when you decide whom to vote for as class president, you make your decision based on criteria.

1. Below are qualities some people have. The list was developed as criteria for choosing a class president. Decide how important you think it is for a president to have each quality. Rank the criteria from 1 to 10 in order of importance. Answers will vary.

_______ is popular with classmates

_______ is able to lead people

_______ is a very organized person

_______ is a good student

_______ has definite ideas about things to change around school

_______ agrees with you on every issue

_______ is attractive

_______ gets along with the teacher

_______ is a hard worker

_______ is considerate of other people

2. Read the descriptions of two students who are running for class president. Decide who you would vote for, based on your ranking of the criteria above. Place an **X** in the box next to that student's description. On the lines following the description, tell why you voted as you did. Answers will vary.

☐ Maria Sanchéz is the top student in class. She gets along well with people, but is not the most popular girl in school. Maria is a hard worker and very well organized. She wants to re-organize part of the school day so that students can spend a few minutes each day doing something for the community—food drives, recycling, and so on. She promises to listen to her classmates' ideas.

____

____

☐ Paul Maki is a good student, but he is not the smartest person in class. He is very popular both with students and with teachers. Paul is tolerant and considerate of all people, and classmates seem to look up to him as a leader. He thinks everything around school is just fine, but he promises he would work hard if he found something that needed changing.

____

____

Name ____

Teacher Note
Discuss pupils' answers. Also discuss how making decisions is not always easy or clear-cut, especially when choosing leaders in a democracy.

Making Decisions

Imagine that you are the manager of a local radio station. A recent poll shows that fewer and fewer people are listening to your station. Listeners are turning the dial to other stations instead. Advertisers—who provide income for your station—are dropping their ads and placing them elsewhere.

A. With a classmate, brainstorm several ways in which you could get evidence that would help you decide what you should do to make the station popular again. List your ideas.

Answers will vary.

B. Now read your list. Check the two ideas that you think would bring in the most helpful information. On the lines below, tell how you would carry out those ideas.

1. Answers will vary.

2.

C. Think ahead. Anticipate a problem you might run into as you collected your evidence. Describe the problem on the lines below.

Answers will vary.

Name

Teacher Note
After pupils have completed the activities and shared their responses, discuss the meaning of the term *original research*, explaining that this is the sort of research the station manager had to do since there were no secondary sources to turn to. Pupils can discuss other situations in which answers can be found only through original research.

Identifying Values

Values are standards of behavior that people think are important. People often have different values, and that might cause a conflict. The story below tells about a value conflict. After you have read the story, answer the questions that follow it.

Julie didn't want to baby-sit for her younger sister and brother, but she had promised her mother to do a good job. Julie knew the rules: only one hour of TV, lots of outdoor exercise, and a healthy lunch. She wondered whether Cora and Tommy would cooperate.

"Wow!" exclaimed Cora. "Since Mom's gone, we can watch TV all day."

"Great!" said Tommy. "I'll make us some lunch and we can eat it in here. We can share a sandwich and save our appetites for ice cream and cookies."

"Forget it!" said Julie. "You know Mom's rules. And I promised to follow them."

"Mom's not here," said Cora. "How's she going to know what we did?"

"Cora's right," said Tommy. "And Julie, I know **you** like TV and ice cream, too. Here is your chance to indulge yourself!"

"Please, Julie," whined Cora. "We'll be on our best behavior if you let us."

Julie thought to herself, "If I don't let Cora and Tommy have their way, they're going to make my day really tough. But if I give in, I'll be breaking my promise to Mom."

1. What do you think Julie should do? Answers will vary. ______________________

____

____

2. How would that decision make her mother feel? Answers will vary. ______________________

____

____

3. How would her decision make Cora and Tommy feel? Answers will vary. ______________________

____

Name ____

Teacher Note
After pupils have compared their responses, discuss the fact that considering how a decision might make other people feel may lead one to change that decision. Have pupils discuss any changes *they* might want to make in *their* decisions after considering their responses to questions 2 and 3.

Identifying Values

The values that many people hold today were set down long ago in sayings and proverbs.

A. Read each old saying. Use your own words to tell what the saying means. Answers will vary.

1. He who hesitates is lost.

2. Better late than never.

3. Haste makes waste.

4. Slow and steady wins the race.

5. Don't put off until tomorrow what you can do today.

B. Read the sayings—and your versions of them—carefully. Do you find that any of the values stated are in conflict? Yes. Explain your answer on the lines below.

Answers will vary but should point out that some of the sayings put a high value on proceeding slowly, and others put a high value on proceeding quickly.

Name

Teacher Note
After pupils have compared their responses, discuss instances in which each of the old sayings might indeed be an accurate evaluation. Pupils will benefit, too, from comparing these sayings to *generalizations*.

Identifying Values

It often happens that a person's **own** values conflict with one another. Read about each person and situation. On the lines, tell **what** you think that person should do, and why you think he or she should do it. Answers will vary.

1. Joel sets a high value on being kind to newcomers. He also sets a high value on playing fair and being a good sport.
   Kirk is a newcomer to school, and Joel, the captain of the kickball team, asks Kirk to join the team. During the very first game, Joel and his teammates notice that Kirk is a poor sport and often cheats. What should Joel, as captain, do?

   ____

   ____

   ____

2. Leon values honesty. He also values doing a good job on his schoolwork. He has been doing poorly in social studies, even though he has spent a lot of time studying.
   Tomorrow is the day of an important social studies test. Leon's friend Gary says, "I saw the teacher put the duplicated copies of the test in her desk drawer, and I'm going to take a copy at recess. Do you want me to get a copy for you, too?" What do you think Leon will do? Why?

   ____

   ____

   ____

3. Allison puts a high value on keeping her promises. She also puts a high value on friendship. Allison promised her little brother that she would take him to the park on Saturday. That morning Allison's friend Cindy calls and says, "Please come over. I feel so blue and need to talk to you alone." What do you think Allison should do? Why?

   ____

   ____

   ____

Name ____

Teacher Note
After pupils have shared their responses, discuss occasions in their own lives when they have had to choose between two or more of their own values.

SKILL 34

Identifying Values

Imagine that it is the year 3000. All Earth people must choose a new planet on which to live. Their choices are the planets Alpha, Beta, or Gamma. Read the descriptions of each planet.

Alpha People do not do physical labor. It is done by machines. Children are raised in nurseries. When they become adults, people work in computer centers or at television broadcasting facilities dedicated to entertainment.

Beta Children are raised at home. Everyone must either attend school or work. All Beta people live exactly the same kind of life. Special awards and prizes, however, are given to citizens who perform special acts for their planet.

Gamma Gamma is known as the old-fashioned planet. Each family has a farm and is expected to provide everything for itself, from food to clothing and housing. There are no schools on Gamma. Children learn their parents' tasks and carry on the work of the farm when they grow up.

A. None of these three planets may suit you exactly. But suppose that you must choose **one** of them as your new home. Which planet would you choose? ____________

Why? Answers will vary.

____

____

B. Name three changes you would like to bring about on the planet you chose.

1. Answers will vary.
2. ______________________________
3. ______________________________

Name ______________________________

Teacher Note
After pupils have shared their responses, discuss the values they would take into consideration when planning "future" projects, such as choosing a career. Encourage pupils to tell about value conflicts that might take place in their own minds as they set about making such choices.

Mood of a Story

A writer builds a **mood**, or feeling, into a story in several ways. One of these ways is to appeal to values and emotions that many of us share. Read the story below. Then complete the activities.

Waiting

Hachi went to a Tokyo railroad station to see his master off to work as usual one day in 1925. At five o'clock, the faithful dog went to meet his master's homecoming train. But that night, his master did not appear and never would again, for he had died during the day.

How was the loyal little dog to know that? Never giving up hope, Hachi went to the railroad station every day for the next ten years and waited for the five o'clock train. When his master did not appear, the dog slunk sadly home again.

The story of the persistent dog spread throughout Japan, and the people came to love this special canine. When Hachi died, the Japanese government built a statue of the dog on the very spot where he had always waited. Tiny replicas of the statue were sent to all the schools in the nation.

1. In the story, find and underline the words or phrases that appeal to values of **affection**, **loyalty**, and **hope**.

2. Circle the phrase that sets a mood of despair or unhappiness.

3. Stories about dogs appeal to a great many people. On the lines below, list some reasons why this may be so.

   Answers will vary.

4. Suppose that you are about to write a story or brief description of a dog. What mood would you try to establish? Answers will vary.

   What words or phrases could you use to establish that mood?

Name

Teacher Note
After pupils have shared their responses, discuss stories and books they have read which set different moods and evoked different feelings in the reader.

Mood of a Story

Writers also establish story mood by carefully constructing descriptions of characters and by giving these characters dialogue that shows the character in action.

Read each paragraph below. On the line before each paragraph, write a word from the box that best describes the character's mood or personality.

curious	ashamed	worried	grateful	kindhearted	angry

angry 1. Vern pounded his fist on the table as he yelled at his brother. "How many times have I told you not to touch my experiment? You've ruined it! Now I'll have to start all over again," said Vern.

ashamed 2. Sadie hung her head. "How could I have been so careless? Now none of you can go to the play, because I forgot to get the tickets. I'm so sorry," she said.

worried 3. Owen walked to the window again and looked out at the storm. "I still don't see anyone coming down the road. The storm is getting worse. I hope they can get home safely," he said.

kindhearted 4. Ellen noticed a young boy sitting alone at the edge of the playground. She went over to him and suggested, "Come and join us. We're going to play dodge ball. If that isn't your favorite, we could play another game later."

curious 5. Jesse purposely chose a seat in the cafeteria beside the new student. Before he even put his tray down, Jesse asked eagerly, "I hear you went to school in South America. What was it like? Which sports did you play?"

grateful 6. "Yes, it's my book. Thank you for bringing it to me. I'm glad you noticed it on the counter, because it was a present and I'm still reading it," said Lois to the stranger who had stopped her as she was leaving the store.

Name ______________________________

Teacher Note
After pupils have checked their responses, ask them to suggest ways in which each selection could be reworded to convey another mood. For example, how could the first selection be changed to make Vern seem worried rather than angry?

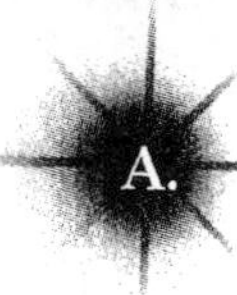

A. Judging Accuracy Making Decisions

This picture appeared in many newspapers all around the world in 1934. Study the picture for clues that will help you answer the questions below.

1. How can you tell that this is a birthday party?

   There are candles on the cake

2. In what way do these five girls seem special?

   They are sisters; they look the same age; they are dressed alike.

3. Suppose you are asked to find evidence to support your answer to question 2. What sources could you use?

   Suggestions: Look in newspaper files for special events of 1934; ask a parent or grandparent if they know the children in the picture.

B. Testing Generalizations

Study the following generalization. Then rewrite it to make it valid.

All children who are special get a lot of publicity and extra attention.

Answers will vary but should mention that many children are special and do not get worldwide attention.

Name

Teacher Note
After pupils have completed part A, discuss their responses. Then explain that these girls were the famous Dionne quintuplets, achieving their fame because they were the first recorded set of quintuplets to reach maturity. Have pupils complete part B and compare their responses.

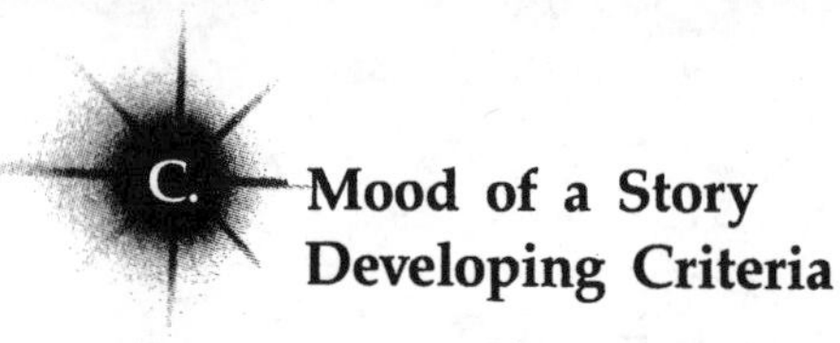

C. Mood of a Story
Developing Criteria

Read the poem. Then complete the activities that follow it.

Mama Is a Sunrise

When she comes slip-footing through the door,
she kindles us
like lump coal lighted,
and we wake up glowing.
She puts a spark even in Papa's eyes
and turns out all our darkness.

When she comes sweet-talking in the room,
she warms us
like grits and gravy,
and we rise up shining.
Even at night-time Mama is a sunrise
that promises tomorrow and tomorrow.

—Evelyn Tooley Hunt

1. Write a sentence that describes the mood of the poem.

Answers will vary.

2. On the lines below, develop two sets of criteria—one for the "perfect parent" and one for the "perfect child."

Perfect Parent	**Perfect Child**
Answers will vary.	

Name

Teacher Note
After pupils have completed the page, they may discuss their responses with you or with a group of classmates.